ACHIEVING
WEALTH
FOR CANADIANS

ACHIEVING WEALTH
FOR CANADIANS

TED LEVALLIANT

Macmillan Canada
Toronto

Please be advised that this book does not constitute legal, accounting or financial planning advice and is intended only to enlighten the reader. The reader is therefore advised to seek the appropriate legal, accounting and financial planning advice from those qualified in such matters prior to implementing any strategy for reducing taxes or achieving wealth.

Canadian Cataloguing in Publication Data

LeValliant, Ted, date.
    Achieving wealth for Canadians

ISBN 0-7715-9033-4

1. Finance, Personal – Canada. 2. Saving and Investment – Canada. 3. Financial Security. I. Title.

HG 179.L48 1994   332.024′.01   C93-095486-6

1 2 3 4 5 BG 98 97 96 95 94

Book designed by Joe Lobo

Cover design by David Wyman
Author Photo by Andrews-Newton Photographers Ltd.

Macmillan Canada wishes to thank the Canada Council and the Ontario Ministry of Culture and Communications for supporting its publishing program.

Macmillan Canada
A Division of Canada Publishing Corporation
Toronto, Ontario, Canada

Printed in Canada

To Margaret, Andy and Holly

ACKNOWLEDGEMENTS

I WISH TO THANK MY WIFE, Margaret, for her support, encouragement and assistance through the many months it took to write this book. I also wish to thank my editor, Susan Girvan of Macmillan Canada, for her invaluable suggestions and insightful editing of the form and substance of this book. Special thanks to Kelly Coyne for word processing and illustrating this document so competently.

I wish to acknowledge and thank Wayne Woods of Woods & Associates, actuarial consultants in Ottawa, who provided the actuarial tables set out in Chapter 5 for Individual Pension Plans.

CONTENTS

PART I
What Is Going On?

PART II
What Are You Going To Do?

PART III
Managing Wealth – Coping With Success.

INTRODUCTION

BOOKS ON FINANCIAL PLANNING ABOUND THESE DAYS. There are more than ever before. Why is this? In a nutshell, Canadians are coming to realize that the financial world we live in is changing around us, increasing the pressure on us to act now to ensure our long-term financial security. It would be a serious mistake to fail to become informed and fail to take positive action.

With a few notable exceptions, however, books on this subject canvass a wide range of investment opportunities, from stocks to bonds, and tax strategies from RRSPs to credits and deductions. Typically, a little bit is written on each of a host of subjects.

This book is different. It zeros in on three basic, powerful wealth building strategies for turning a middle to upper income into financial independence.

Underlying this book is a philosophy for achieving wealth in Canada. Although this philosophy will be of interest to those at all income levels, it is particularly applicable to those with middle to upper incomes.

Please be advised that this book does not constitute legal, accounting or financial planning advice and is intended only to enlighten the reader. The reader is therefore advised to seek the appropriate legal, accounting and financial planning advice from those qualified in such matters prior to implementing any strategy for reducing taxes or achieving wealth.

This book is aimed in particular at those who have yet to take seriously the task of providing for their long-term financial security, whether that failure to act is due to a lack of information, procrastination or a mistaken belief that it cannot be done.

Ted LeValliant
Ottawa, Canada

PROLOGUE

*The Tale of the
Impoverished Dentist*

THIS IS THE TALE OF HARRY D.F.B. DENTIST, practicing out of a rented but well equipped office in a small satellite community near Heavy Plant, Ontario.

Harry is by no means atypical. He is 53 years of age and has been practicing dentistry near Heavy Plant for 24 years. Harry's wife, Dolly, formerly a dental hygienist but now the dental office manager, works full-time in the practice.

Dolly runs the show, and that includes the staff of six: two full-time hygienists, one part-time hygienist, two dental assistants and a receptionist. Dolly keeps the books, controls Harry's schedule and handles the myriad of dental industry and non-dental industry salespeople who descend on Harry's office every day.

Harry is a successful dental practitioner. He has gross billings of about $350,000 every year, more like $500,000 when the gross billings of the hygienists are included, although this gross billing level has been declining a little each year of late. Harry has the respect of his colleagues because of these billing levels, generated from a full range of dental services and a larger than average chunk of crown, bridge and restorative work, lucrative procedures when you have the skill to perform them efficiently, which Harry does.

Harry has no other dentist, partner or associate working with him in his practice and never has, although an orthodontist from Heavy Plant comes in once a week as necessary. But this will soon change when Harry and Dolly's daughter, Debbie, joins the practice next year after she completes her dental studies at McGill University. Debbie is 26.

Harry and Dolly want the best, of course, for Debbie. They hope that she will work into the practice and that as Harry gets older he will be able to phase out, eventually working only one or two days a week and then retiring, leaving the practice to Debbie. Harry and Dolly used to talk about retirement at 55 but it now looks as if the early to mid-60s will be more like it.

You see, Harry and Dolly haven't managed to build a lot of wealth for retirement. How could this be, you ask, when their gross income is so high? What happened to their money?

Well, first of all, although $500,000 in gross billings may seem like an awful lot, the expenses of running a dental practice are very high. Six salaries add up. Rent and equipment are expensive. And then there's the cost of malpractice insurance, bills to the dental lab for lab work, accounting fees and on and on. Try as she might, Dolly has been unable to get the total expenses below $320,000 a year in recent times, leaving a net income of $180,000 for Harry and Dolly. Dolly takes $40,000 for her full-time efforts and Harry takes $140,000. This is the split recommended by their accountant, Dick, a rather conservative fellow by nature.

But then there is income tax, a wealth destroyer for sure. In rough numbers, Harry paid $50,000 last year and Dolly paid

$10,000, for a total of $60,000. This left Harry and Dolly with a combined net total of $120,000, $10,000 a month to live on and to provide for retirement. It sounds like a lot, doesn't it? Certainly upper income rather than middle income. So why aren't Harry and Dolly already in a position to retire? Aren't they already wealthy enough?

These are good questions. The answers may surprise you. First, although Harry and Dolly control office expenses to the penny, they plop the $10,000 they draw out each month into their chequing account and spend it as they wish to run their home, pay the cost of Debbie's university education and enjoy themselves.

And at the end of the month there may be a thousand or two left in the chequing account. Sometimes the balance gets up to $20,000 or $30,000 or more—earning not a penny of interest, mind you.

Harry and Dolly own their home, a beautiful Cape Cod with 6,000 square feet on the outskirts of town. It would still have been mortgage-free but for the $150,000 renovation last year. The logic was that this would make a beautiful retirement premises or could be sold at a handsome price if Harry and Dolly decided to move elsewhere on retirement. And in the meantime it would be perfect for entertaining. I would estimate the equity in this home today to be about $275,000.

Harry has managed to accumulate $100,000 in his RRSP and Dolly has $25,000 in hers. Dick has been after them to contribute the maximum (more than $20,000 annually between them) to cut their taxes down, but last year they missed again as a result of cost overruns on the house renovation. Another factor was the general disgust they felt with the whole process of dealing with money matters after learning from their friend and sometime financial adviser, Manny, that the tax shelter they had plunked $50,000 into four years ago—Race Horses Limited Partnership—had collapsed and the money was gone, although they had saved a chunk of tax at the time they purchased the limited partnership units.

Then there's the raw land 75 miles out of town in the middle of nowhere that their friend and real estate agent, Ben, recommended they purchase. Where else in the world (except perhaps in the middle of the Mojave Desert) could you get 60 hectares for $200,000? After all, it's land; they're not making any more of it. It can only go up in value. Never mind that the banker, Bill, would only lend $75,000 without a personal guarantee. It's land, something you can see and touch and sink your heels into. And there's no income tax on it until it's sold at a profit some day down the road.

And then there's the cottage on the river, the expensive speedboat, the two fancy cars, the trips... You get the picture: a range of toys to help Harry and Dolly enjoy the good life and impress the friends and colleagues, easily rationalized as important tools to relieve the stress of an intense career. And why not? From the second year of Harry's dental practice there has always been lots of money. Won't there always be?

Dolly is not sure. She worries that there may not be enough for retirement. She worries about the fact that Harry won't take the medical that their friend and insurance agent, John, has been nagging about so that Harry can increase his life insurance coverage from the measly $350,000 whole life policy he bought 15 years ago. Harry says he's not willing to waste good money on insurance he might never need. And anyway, the real estate mortgages and the $100,000 line of credit for the dental practice are life-insured, aren't they?

Dolly worries that the RRSP isn't really growing. The Canada Savings Bonds that Dick (the conservative accountant) recommended don't seem to be producing much growth. Manny is recommending using the funds for a condo development in the business district of Heavy Plant. Harry likes that idea because it's rooted in the land. The financial services salespeople who descend on dental offices like locusts recommend a wide range of options. Dolly decides repeatedly to decide later. And Harry is so stressed from the intensity of the practice that, when the workday is over, he just wants to relax, which more often than not involves spending a chunk of that hard-earned money.

But the thing that worries Dolly and Harry most is that the dental practice seems to be changing. Gross billings are declining slightly each year. The number of new patients moving into the area is declining. Two of the plants in Heavy Plant have closed and another just announced an indefinite layoff of 180 people, something to do with increased competition from a plant in the Carolinas and the need to add more automation to the plant. Thank goodness Harry is adept at marketing his superb crown and bridge skills.

At recent dental association conventions, Dolly and Harry have heard from a range of tax, financial and dental office management experts that they should modernize certain aspects of the management of the practice to increase profitability, reorganize their tax affairs to cut down the $60,000 they send to the government each year and set in place a financial plan to manage their finances so they can achieve long-term financial security.

But when Harry asked Dick about some of the ideas they'd heard (when Dick dropped by last April 30 with their tax returns and news that a cheque for a further $20,000 would have to be enclosed with Harry's return because the quarterly tax instalments had been too low), Dick didn't seem too enthused. It all sounded a bit complicated to him. And hiring a group of experts would be expensive, particularly at a time when cash flow was poor. Why not wait until things improved before making changes?

Why not indeed? In the first 24 years of the practice Harry and Dolly built a net worth (excluding the practice) of about $750,000 (all assets less all debts). The practice is probably worth somewhere in the neighbourhood of $350,000, so the overall net worth is more like $1.1 million. And Harry still has a number of working years left. Not bad?

Let's look at it. Let's assume that Harry and Dolly sold everything right now, including the home and the practice (presumably to Debbie), and retired to a rented condo. There would be no tax on the sale of the house because it is a principal residence. There would be capital gains tax on the sale of certain other assets. Let's ignore most of the other niceties (and the fact that $125,000 is inside RRSPs) and assume, for simplicity's sake, that Harry and Dolly walk away with $900,000 cash. That's it. No pension, and Old Age Security some years down the road. Will $900,000 be enough to finance their lifestyle?

Assume that Harry and Dolly (who are not investment wizards, as we have seen) get a rate of return in an interest bearing instrument of 7.5%, which is an extremely generous assumption considering their past performance and the fact that rates are low these days. Because they have done no tax planning whatsoever, assume that the entire tax bite from the income generated from the $900,000 will fall in Harry's lap.

The income per year, therefore, would be $67,500 before tax ($900,000 x 7.5%), but after tax that amount would be reduced to about $50,000, approximately $4,000 per month. That's less than half the amount Harry and Dolly spend now per month but still a nice income by the standards of most Canadians.

The alarming thing, however, is that with an annual inflation rate of, say, 4% per year (a realistic assumption, as explained in subsequent chapters), the purchasing power of $4,000 a month today would, 10 years from now, be reduced to $2,650. How will Harry and Dolly enjoy living on $2,650 a month when Harry is 63? I have an even better question. How will they enjoy $1,750 a month when Harry is 73, $1,200 a month when Harry is 83, $750 a month when Harry is 93? They won't.

Harry and Dolly will certainly need the Canada Pension and Old Age Security in a big way. Hopefully, the Canadian social assistance net will still be there to catch them.

But what a travesty! Here is a professional couple with $500,000 a year in gross income and $180,000 a year in net income. And to need social assistance, to be below the poverty line however you define it, to be poor—no, impoverished—in the golden years!

The tragedy appears all the greater when you realize that, had Harry and Dolly set aside from the beginning a modest amount monthly and invested it wisely according to the strategies set out in this book, Harry could retire today and Harry and Dolly would never have to worry about being impoverished.

As it is, it is obvious that Harry and Dolly cannot retire. They must work as long as they can. Even if they do, their future financial security will never be assured as long as they continue to behave in a financially irresponsible manner, taking bad advice and avoiding coming to grips with basic financial and tax planning issues.

But I happen to know Harry and Dolly personally. From my perspective as a lawyer with an interest in tax planning and as a person interested in wealth accumulation, I have tried to highlight for them the need to take positive action to prevent a potential disaster.

At first I wasn't getting through; the defense mechanisms kicked in. It would mean change. They'd always had lots of money, so how could it ever get that bad? Harry hates dealing with this sort of thing. It would cost a lot. Why hadn't Dick pointed out the problem? Maybe they should wait until the future of Heavy Plant unfolded a little more? They'd decide later, but soon.

Well, the thing that got Harry and Dolly moving was the pending graduation of Debbie from dental college. She is at the beginning of her career and has everything ahead of her. She is starting when taxes are high and the future of Heavy Plant is more uncertain than ever before. If she plans her affairs intelligently from the outset, however, she could avoid Harry and Dolly's predicament. She could even achieve wealth and retire early.

Absolutely. But it is by no means too late for Harry and Dolly. As they warmed to the idea of restructuring the dental practice for Debbie's sake, they began to see that long-term financial security is also well within their grasp.

PART
I

What Is Going On?

1

Building Wealth
– Can We Talk?

MY FRIEND HARRY IS NOT UNUSUAL. Millions of dollars pass through the hands of many Canadians during their working lives, but nearly all of these people fail to achieve wealth. Is this because achieving wealth and financial security is impossible? Or can it be done?

Now, I am an optimist, but also a realist, and one must be both to build wealth in Canada these days. An optimist believes in the possible. A realist faces facts, confronts challenges squarely, recognizes a spade and calls it what it is.

The financial climate that Harry and Dolly and the rest of us live in is a tough one. Canadian taxes are very high. Our governments are insolvent by any reasonable definition of that term. Our economy is in transition, but to what? We face declining demand for our traditional raw materials; both our industrial plants and our population are aging and global competition is here, including competition from countries less committed to our social and environmental values.

All this bad news and uncertainty has put many Canadians in a dour mood, made us insecure, uncertain about the future and what it may hold. Little wonder there is a lack of business and consumer confidence and the popular belief is that any recoveries will be little more than diversions on the road to a new economic order, one that is evolving slowly and is at least five, 10 or 15 years away.

Most Canadians understand that there is a tremendous restructuring under way—I call this the Great Restructuring—as one economic era decays and a new one emerges. And Canadians are correct in their belief that we are only partway through the Great Restructuring and that more change, significant change, is yet to come.

It's a tough time to be optimistic about building wealth; it's even tough to be a realist and brave the issues, especially when there's so much emphasis on the negative. But it is possible to do both; moreover, it is a must.

The news of our shrinking economy and less than rosy prospects may make the idea of achieving wealth today seem far-fetched. It looks like we've lost our window of opportunity. But now the news takes a strange turn: even during the boom years of the last few decades (the "good old days") only one Canadian in 10 set in motion a plan to build personal financial security in any meaningful way. Only 50% of the population contributed to an RRSP, with most falling well short of the maximum possible contributions.

Even in the roaring 1980s, when there was lots of money around and lots of opportunities, only 10% of Canadians were taking the steps necessary to achieve this objective. Of the remaining 90%, many apparently planned to live solely on family and government assistance when they got older or simply chose to ignore the issue.

The punch line is that those numbers have not changed in the sober, more restrained 1990s. Notwithstanding the challenges presented by the Great Restructuring, 10% of Canadians are still busy building personal financial security. The rest still assume that tomorrow will take care of itself or there will be a miracle or sufficient government assistance will be available when the days of earning income are over.

There are those among us who are less fortunate and who, for a variety of legitimate reasons, must look to family and the state for financial assistance. But those of us with revenue streams that are average and above average—who will have had a few million dollars pass through our hands during our earning years—continue to squander the opportunities that knock on our door every day. What opportunities, you ask? Didn't I just say that times are changing?

Times are changing but opportunities remain. The fact is that many Canadians simply lack the understanding of wealth accumulation required to take advantage of the opportunities that exist. But don't forget that 10% of us have figured out how to go about building personal financial security; if we make as much money as they do (or more) we should be able to do the same. When I talk about "personal financial security" I mean building wealth sufficient to allow you to do those things you reasonably want to do, even if you live to a ripe old age; enough money to generate the income necessary to maintain the standard of living to which you have reasonably become accustomed. I am aware that personal financial security means different things to different people, but this is what I mean when I use the term. Whatever financial security means to you, if you are in the middle to upper income range, you have the means to secure it. And opportunities—different opportunities from the ones in the 1980s—still exist.

Now, making any decision to take advantage of these opportunities is often clouded by a nagging suspicion that setting out to achieve wealth and building personal financial security is inherently evil or at least inappropriate, smacking of greed, materialism and the like—perhaps based on the belief that for someone to gain, someone else must inevitably lose. Popular opinion disdains those who set out to become wealthy. Having wealth thrust upon us through lottery winnings or an inheritance is considered perfectly acceptable, but working steadily toward wealth indicates an unhealthy state of mind.

This school of thought is misguided. Most of us know that money isn't everything—family, health and spiritual happiness are more important. But personal financial security is also a worthwhile objective, one that can enhance your opportunity to live life to the fullest.

Achieving that objective is always a challenge because of a mixture of our basic human nature and a smattering of ignorance. Look at Harry and Dolly—they're busy people who tend to procrastinate when it comes to issues that are long-term and seem complicated and rife with uncertainty. Don't we all prefer to begin to build wealth tomorrow rather than today?

The smattering of ignorance is, from my experience, not so much a lack of the ability to understand interest rates, stocks, bonds, RRSPs, mutual funds, inflation, tax laws and the like as a fundamental lack of understanding of the concept of transforming a revenue stream into wealth. We saw that millions of dollars will flow through Harry and Dolly's hands and that the pool of wealth at the end of the process will be too small to sustain them. What is the concept that they (and many of us) have missed? It's the idea that you can divert some of your resources through tax planning and other sensible means, and then redirect those resources to investments that will grow enough to outpace the ravages of taxes and inflation.

The lack of understanding of how wealth is created is intertwined with the suspicion that it can't be done (or if it can be done, it's going to be no fun at all, and maybe downright unpleasant). Most middle to upper income Canadians honestly believe that it's impossible to build financial independence, or they believe that there's no point in trying to do so because taxes and inflation will take it all away, and that furthermore the short-term pain of doing without many things they want or need would be too great to bear. The typical Canadian response to a discussion of serious financial management goes something like this:

> "I don't really believe I can organize my affairs to achieve wealth, at least not without undergoing ridiculous hardship. On my earnings and with my cost of living, there's no way I can accomplish that objective. If I thought there was, I'd get started."

This widely held view, coupled with "I'm too old to start now," "I'm too young, I can wait" and other reasons, is paralysing. And it will doom you to the cash-poor or never-get-ahead status quo. You can do better.

I believe to the soles of my shoes that it's well within the realm of possibility (no, probability) for most of us with a middle to upper revenue stream to build substantial wealth without destroying our standard of living.

It's worth noting, by the way, that by world standards middle to upper income Canadians live well. We're good consumers, spending as we go. We often own our homes and have either a pension plan or an RRSP, or both, notwithstanding that we may pay little attention to either. We spend much and save some. We own a lot of assets, mostly of the depreciating variety such as automobiles, furnishings, electronic gadgets and the like, often with personal debt to match. Most of us also pay a significant chunk in taxes. Many would praise us as the engines of our economy, keeping money in circulation and pouring it into government coffers.

I have a somewhat different point of view. I believe that accumulating wealth through wise investing is better for the economy than endless consumption. It is the key to your own personal prosperity and a key to the prosperity of the country as a whole. Putting all of those hard-earned dollars to work throughout the economy, in stocks and bonds and interest bearing instruments, provides the funds for corporations to grow and create employment and the funds for the financing of all sorts of economic development. And your personal financial security is enhanced in the process. It's not that spending, saving, borrowing and paying taxes aren't good for the economy, it's just that investing and accumulating personal wealth are better.

Historically, Canadians have had a strong tendency to save or spend but not to put money to work by investing. As a people we should invest more; we should put our capital to work.

Encouraging Canadians to invest and encouraging them to become financially independent is not a matter of encouraging the rich to become richer while the poor inevitably become poorer. In fact, putting all that money to work in productive ways will, I believe, assist our industries and our work force to reposition, retool and retrain to meet the challenges of the Great Restructuring.

From your own personal perspective, the challenge is to achieve financial security. Is this possible? How can it be accomplished? Where should you start? The answers to these questions are discussed in the pages ahead.

It's true that the earlier you begin or the greater your earnings, the easier the task of wealth building becomes. But it's literally never too late to begin, and any reasonable level of income will suffice. I wish to point out, however, that while this book focuses on three basic and powerful principles that apply to everyone, the strategies suggested here will particularly benefit those with better incomes. If you find this intriguing, read on.

2

THE GREAT RESTRUCTURING

And Other Economic Complications

A S A PROSPECTIVE INVESTOR, there are some things you need to know about your economic environment. We live in the denouement of the 20th century, but it's the denouement of more than that. Average Canadians understand that we are living at the end of a prosperous Canadian economic era based on the extraction of abundant raw materials and the manufacture of goods for domestic consumption behind protectionist walls.

Whether we like it or not, a Great Restructuring is under way. Traditional manufacturing businesses in Canada are being replaced by companies working in information-based technologies, businesses that must compete internationally to survive. We have the resources to do this; the Great Restructuring is not the end of us. However, it is a shame that we must make this transition loaded to the gunwales with debt.

Debt

Spurred by the consumerism that followed two world wars and the rise of new and powerful economies built by young populations, this century has seen a period of prosperity unprecedented in Western history.

That prosperity, however, began to smack of illusion in the final quarter of the century in Canada and elsewhere as governments at all levels, together with corporations and individuals, racked up debt at equally unprecedented levels, debt that will be extremely difficult for future generations to repay. It was once assumed that the economy was capable of infinite growth and that such growth would outrun any debt we accumulated. This assumption seemed logical 20, even 10 years ago, but times have changed. Growth has slowed and debt is piling up, partly because of the same compound growth characteristics that, as will be explained, will work in your favour as you set out on the road to personal wealth accumulation. Governments are caught in a vicious circle as planned levels of expenditure remain unchanged while revenues shrink. At the same time, the restructuring must be financed as workers retrain or are left behind. At present, if federal, provincial and municipal annual deficits are combined, we are slipping into debt at the rate of approximately $2,000 a second! That's a lot of debt to outgrow or outrun.

As the world's largest debtor nation on a per capita basis, Canada has a serious challenge ahead of it. Our future will depend in part on getting this debt under control at all levels. This includes government debt, corporate debt and individual debt. Canadians in general must stop living beyond their means and planning to pay for everything later. This is mortgaging the future. Down deep, I believe, we all understand this. If we can substantially reduce the liabilities that are draining our individual and collective resources and take advantage of our brain power and advanced infrastructures, we can compete effectively in this changing world. The only things that will stop us are a lack of deficit and debt reduction and a failure to focus our energies on the tools necessary to make the transition: research and development, education and new management skills to guide the transition. A general disbelief among many of us that we have a role to play in both debt reduction and the Great Restructuring will also keep us (and future generations) from meeting this challenge.

In contemporary Canada, prosperity is not a birthright. As hewers of wood and drawers of water (and more recently borrowers of money), many Canadians have come to believe that it is. The rude awakening is under way.

The Global Marketplace

Fortunately, a new breed of Canadian business person is competing successfully in the emerging global economy. But while it may be that this sector is on its way to replacing our traditional economy and putting us back on the road to prosperity, the transition from one type of economy to another is causing displacement and upheaval.

One response is to build a wall around Canada, to keep manufacturing in and global competition out. We did this for years and for a time the strategy gave us a lucrative industrial base. But now others can produce the same goods more cheaply and trade barriers are falling around the world. If we have any doubts about the strategy in today's world, we need only look at Brazil, where the computer industry demanded and obtained barriers to keep out foreign computer competition and preserve jobs. Jobs were indeed protected but the industry developed in isolation and the result was an expensive technology unable to communicate effectively with the technologies in the rest of the world. Short-term jobs became a long-term liability. No, protectionism is no longer the answer. In an era of high technology and instant communications it is practically impossible to isolate a nation from global forces. In this regard, it's important to realize that the restructuring is not ours alone. It's happening in all of the industrialized nations and affects developing countries as well. The answer to global restructuring is to look outward, not inward.

But what will become of us (and our prosperity) as the manufacturing jobs move elsewhere? The answer, a painful one while we are in transition, is that, as a nation, we will learn to be competitive in the manufacturing industries we retain and we will find other ways to earn our living.

As individuals, I believe that many (though not all) of us will adapt. Displaced managers, executives, professionals, those with entrepreneurial skills or those willing and able to acquire them, those in the technologies and others are beginning to appreciate that the world of the 21st century will belong to skilled, entrepreneurial Canadians who can take advantage of global opportunities as never before. Rather than waiting for the traditional engines of the economy to restart, those of us who cannot take part directly in the restructuring must be prepared to nurture the change or else watch the prosperity of all Canadians continue to decline.

Yes, "continue" is the operative word. You have no doubt noticed that your standard of living has become more difficult to maintain in the past few years. The standard of living of Canadians has in fact been in decline since the late 1980s.

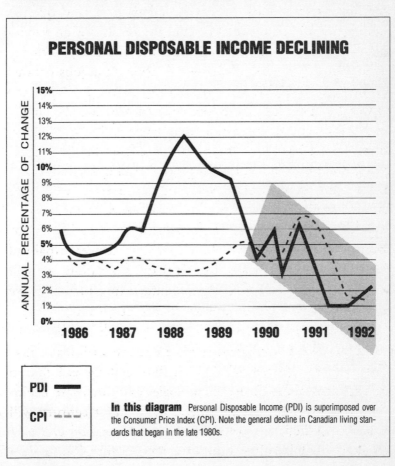

PERSONAL DISPOSABLE INCOME DECLINING

PDI ━━━

CPI - - -

In this diagram Personal Disposable Income (PDI) is superimposed over the Consumer Price Index (CPI). Note the general decline in Canadian living standards that began in the late 1980s.

The Road Ahead

What does this tangled web of debt and change mean to you? First, I believe that it means that the "good old days" are gone, forever. Historians will probably look back at this transition and consider it to have been an economic revolution as significant as the industrial revolution in its day, indeed a Great Restructuring. What lies ahead? Fundamental changes in the way many of us earn our living and the way governments manage their economies. It may be increasingly difficult for us to maintain social programs such as Medicare and Old Age Security *in their current, familiar forms.* These programs were developed to serve the needs and conditions of times that are disappearing. New approaches will evolve either by choice or necessity. New, cost-effective approaches that assist those in most need will be the hallmark of Canadian social programs of the future. Basic Canadian principles of fairness and generosity will hopefully not be betrayed but the delivery of these programs may well be modified. How will that affect those of us in the best position to take care of ourselves? Perhaps the issue of personal wealth accumulation is about to assume more importance in our lives.

I predict that if we choose to pretend that this shift is not happening and try to conduct our personal, corporate and national business as usual, Canadian taxes will go higher and higher. And I predict that if we persist in our support of politicians at all levels who deny the inevitable and believe that it is acceptable to continue to spend more money than is taken in, we'll see the return of succession or death taxes in a number of provinces over the years ahead, taking from the rich and giving to the poor—or at least taking from the rich to feed the apparently endless appetite of Canadian governments.

Sales taxes, consumption taxes, user fees, claw-backs, property taxes and a host of other taxes, not the least of which are income taxes, will be the order of the day, likely coupled with decreasing services across the land as servicing debt becomes the all-consuming budget item. This is not some doomsday prediction. The process is already under way, and all of us sense this when we read a newspaper or listen to a newscast. Moves to take more from the rich ostensibly to give to the poor are almost inevitable but they will force us to surrender our fates (as well as our cash) to governments that will absorb resources better put to use elsewhere.

So what's the answer? In theory it's really quite simple: collectively we must stop mortgaging our country's future. We must identify our strengths as they relate to the new, information-based industries and work together to participate effectively in the global economy. This includes refocusing our education system, retraining the work force as necessary, sponsoring research and development, ensuring that our infrastructures (roads, airports and the like) do not deteriorate and making sure that those sectors with the best chance of competing internationally are not held back.

It sounds so obvious and so simple. But Canadians know that it's not. We know that we have too many levels of government, provincial trade barriers are often greater than those between Canada and its major trading partners and there is a general dependency on government and on the money that has traditionally flowed from accessible raw materials.

But how can the individual Canadian with a middle to upper income affect any of this? Must we care that the

Canadian economy faces a daunting array of challenges from within and without? Clearly the answer is yes. As Canadians, we have a collective interest in continuing the Canadian success story for future generations. As individuals, we're more likely to build wealth if we're aware of the trends and the challenges we face.

I am optimistic that collectively we will emerge from the Great Restructuring with a new, revitalized economy, one able to compete effectively on the global stage. What are the underpinnings of this optimism? First, my belief in the resourcefulness and determination of the Canadian people. Then, the solid base we have on which to build: technology, financial and educational institutions, research facilities, stable government and the like. In this regard we're the envy of the world.

But financing our economy's revitalization will require huge pools of private sector capital. And where better to find it than in the hands of individual Canadians like you, not by taking it from you in taxes but by encouraging you to multiply the resources at your disposal, to accumulate wealth for your own benefit and the benefit of us all.

Aging Population

My generation—the baby boomers—is soon to swell the ranks of senior citizenry in unprecedented numbers, and its members have a flair for life and a lot of demands. As a group we've made a dramatic impact on everything we've touched, from the baby food industry in the 1950s to the music industry in the 1960s to the consumerism of the 1970s to the borrowing of the 1980s and the home office phenomenon of the 1990s. We crowded into the universities, built huge homes in sprawling suburbs and otherwise changed Canadian society as no group ever has before.

But there's more to come. As we move into our golden years, we could bankrupt our social security system unless bold steps at all levels are taken to prevent this from happening. On an individual level, the very best step you can take to avoid the impact of such a disaster is tax effective financial planning and wealth creation. And this individual action will have national implications.

In my view, nothing could be better for our prospects than hundreds of thousands of Canadians accumulating wealth through investment.

But the growing number of senior citizens is by no means the end of the story. Even if there weren't such a large group of us heading to retirement, increasing longevity would still pose financial planning challenges. Canadians are living longer, healthier lives. The emphasis on fitness, as well as increasing medical knowledge and technological capabilities, are creating a new wave of active seniors who want more out of life.

Assuming a life span of 90 years (which is the life span sometimes used today for calculating annuities and the like, despite the fact that medical advances and healthier lifestyles have yet to see the average Canadian reach that age), the life of a typical Canadian can be divided into three phases:

- the formative years and career launch: ages 0 to 30;
- the middle or earning years: ages 31 to 60;
- the golden or retirement years: ages 61 to 90.

This division highlights something quite startling. The huge baby boom invasion of the golden, retirement years will see increasing numbers of Canadians spending one-third of

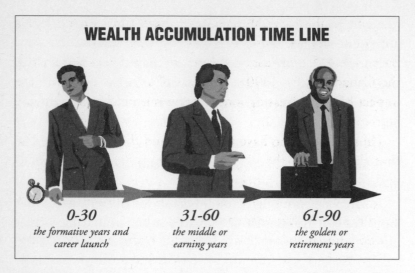

WEALTH ACCUMULATION TIME LINE

0-30
the formative years and
career launch

31-60
the middle or
earning years

61-90
the golden or
retirement years

their lives in that phase. Although many baby boomers plan to retire in their 50s, I suspect that many will work longer, at least part-time, both of financial necessity and as a result of a shortage of skilled personnel in the fields of management and the technologies. But increased years of retirement will nevertheless be the norm as a result of increased longevity.

It used to be that planning for retirement involved planning for five or 10 or maybe 15 years. But planning for 20 or 30 years or more is a very different thing.

What tools do we have to deal with the coming crunch? Many of us have put our faith in RRSPs, but socking the maximum into an RRSP and doing a good job of looking after it is not a complete solution to this conundrum, particularly for those of us in middle age. Far too many Canadians believe that it is. And an employer-sponsored pension plan is no longer a complete answer, particularly if its benefits are not fully indexed to inflation.

As we've already established, the boom times of the 1980s are gone, and we must stop denying that the fundamental economic order has changed forever. Such denial abounds in the Canada of the 1990s, and part of it is the denial of the impact of our increasing longevity on our need to accumulate personal wealth.

Those of you who have moved beyond this denial to realize that the rules of the game have changed are beginning to understand that to provide properly for long-term financial security you must build more wealth than you ever imagined you'd need. The light has come on.

The questions that will logically occur to you in this enlightened state are the ones we talked about in Chapter 1. Is it possible for an individual Canadian on a middle to upper income to build enough wealth to meet the challenge? How great will the sacrifice, if any, have to be? How do I go about it? We'll pursue the answers to these questions in the coming chapters.

3

WHAT HAPPENED TO YOUR MONEY?

Wealth Destroyers and Wealth Builders

IN MY EXPERIENCE, QUICK AND EASY MONEY is a long and difficult time in the making. Our dentist friend from the prologue knows this too. To have millions pass through our hands and end up relying on government assistance tells us that wealth doesn't just happen. Short of winning a lottery or robbing a bank, I know of no get-rich-quick scheme you can rely on.

No, quick and easy money is hard to come by and has little to do with transforming a middle to upper income stream into wealth over the longer term. The key to wealth creation for most Canadians, including those who own their own businesses, professionals, independent contractors and employees, is to follow the strategies set out in this book, to build wealth over the medium to long term.

TAXES, INFLATION AND COMPOUND GROWTH

To go straight to the nub of the issue, the key to achieving wealth for those with a middle to upper-level income is to free up and invest some income in a tax sheltered way so that the rate of return exceeds applicable taxes and the rate of inflation. The goal is to enable the funds invested to double in size repeatedly so that significant wealth can be accumulated.

Taxes

Never underestimate the effect of taxes on your financial welfare. At the individual level, Canadians are among the most highly taxed people in the world. And taxes are generally on the rise, not on the decline. The degree of taxation is a matter of national concern. That said, I believe that it is your duty as a Canadian taxpayer to organize your affairs in such a manner that the least tax legally required will be paid. Many Canadians pay more tax than they should and I believe that this is detrimental, not just for them but for the country as a whole.

I believe that a dollar invested wisely in the private sector will create more wealth and more employment than the same dollar placed in the hands of government. First, a private sector dollar will tend to circulate more quickly through the economy and therefore give more bang for the buck. Second, a private sector dollar is more likely to be attracted to an activity in line with Canada's future while a government dollar is more likely to be put to work preserving the old economic order. In other words, every time government removes a dollar from the private sector, and particularly when it spends it attempting to preserve the past, there is one less dollar available to make the transition already under way in the Great Restructuring.

Taxes, they say, are as inevitable as death itself, but there are really three inevitabilities when it comes to accumulating wealth: death, taxes and inflation. All three must be taken into account, although I'll deal with death later. While I will point out in the next chapter the enormous difference, for example, between a 12% and a 15% rate of return in the wealth accumulation process, if one-quarter or one-half of that return is taxed away and a percentage of the rest is eaten by inflation, those rates of return are largely illusionary. Let's assume that you earn a rate of 12% per year. If taxes take 50%, you are left with a 6% rate of return, and if inflation erodes your buying power by 4%, only 2% is left. Your 12% annual rate of return has shrunk sixfold to 2%. What a depressing thought! You can use a financial calculator all day long and not overcome that one.

But things could be worse. Take the example of someone who purchases a Canada Savings Bond in a taxable environment (outside a tax sheltering vehicle such as an RRSP). A low risk investment, right? Assume the bond pays 7%, that the tax bracket is roughly 50% and inflation is 4%. The after-tax rate of return is 3.5%. If you then deduct the 4% for inflation, the actual rate of return is in fact a loss of .5% per year. Projected over a long enough period, therefore, all of the investor's buying power will disappear. Low risk indeed!

It is obvious, therefore, that you must have a better strategy than this to build any amount of wealth. Higher returns are essential. Proper tax planning is a must.

It's amazing how few Canadians really understand or do anything about these important realities, how few have proper tax and financial planning or any sort of overall strategy. Few believe that, using proper strategies, significant wealth can be accumulated from a good revenue stream. The starting point is good tax planning.

You can either save taxes today or, just as important, defer taxes to tomorrow, or both. Because taxes in Canada play a tremendous role as a wealth destroyer, and because of the technical discussion we need to have to come to grips with them, I will treat various aspects of taxes in some depth.

Income taxes were introduced in Canada by the Income War Tax Act as a temporary measure in 1917 to assist in paying the cost of the First World War. Once introduced, however, income taxes grew and grew and became permanent.

The Canadian income tax system was revised substantially in the early 1970s and, in the jargon used in the United States, there was "tax reform" in the 1980s.

What there has not been in any way, shape or form is tax simplification. Despite lip service paid to this concept, Canada's tax laws have become more and more complex over the decades since they were first introduced. The present Income Tax Act and Regulations, moreover, contain hundreds of sections, subsections, paragraphs, subparagraphs, clauses, subclauses and even sub-subclauses. There are Revenue Canada policy statements, generally in the form of Interpretation Bulletins and Information Circulars, together with thousands of court cases interpreting the various provisions.

While it is fair to say that very few Canadians understand our income tax laws well, it is also fair to say that the underlying tax policies, at least to the extent they involve the raising of revenues, are rather straightforward. In fact, if the Income Tax Act and Regulations were used only to raise revenues, Canadian income tax laws would be much simpler than they are.

The difficulty is that successive Canadian governments have used tax law as an instrument of social and economic policy, not just to raise revenues. For example, tax law has been used to encourage a variety of activities, including the making of Canadian films and research and development. Although no doubt noble pursuits in their own right, these social and economic policy matters clutter and confuse Canadian tax laws in a major way.

As a result of tax reform, the multiplicity of different tax brackets in Canada was reduced to three. The three remaining tax brackets are approximately 25%, 40% and 50% of taxable income when both federal and provincial income taxes are combined. For simplicity, these three approximate tax rates will be used throughout this book.

The word used to describe Canada's income tax system is "progressive." This means that generally, the higher your income, the higher your tax bracket. Those in the lowest tax bracket pay 25% of every dollar they earn, once they have exhausted available credits and deductions. Those with a taxable income in excess of approximately $30,000 pay tax at the 25% rate up to $30,000 and then enter the middle tax bracket and pay 40% of dollars earned above that level. Those with a taxable income in excess of about $60,000 pay tax at the 25% rate up to $30,000, 40% from $30,000 to $60,000 and then enter the top tax bracket and pay 50% of dollars earned above $60,000.

Traditionally, the progressivity of the tax system for individuals was indexed to inflation. When inflation was say, 4%, the tax system was adjusted 4% accordingly so that a taxpayer was not drawn into a higher tax bracket for the next dollar earned merely as a result of the impact of inflation. Since 1988, however, personal tax credits and tax brackets have been indexed only to the extent the Consumer Price Index increases annually by more than 3%. In other words, if inflation is 4%, only the excess above 3%, namely 1%, is indexed.

This partial de-indexation of the tax system was and is a powerful provision that received little publicity when it was instituted. The upshot of it is obvious. A certain number of taxpayers in the lowest and middle tax brackets have their top dollar of taxable income pulled up into the next higher bracket each year there is inflation even if their taxable incomes have not increased. In other words, they get a little poorer.

And there is no guarantee that the highest tax bracket—the 50% marginal tax rate—will not be increased over the years ahead. I predict that there will be considerable political pressure to increase taxes for those in the upper tax bracket in an effort to redistribute wealth in this country.

There are other pressures on our income tax system in Canada. The first is that the income tax system is hemorrhaging, failing to pull in tax dollars as efficiently as it used to. This is because in the "good old days" a greater percentage of the Canadian work force was on the payroll of larger corporations than is the case today. Most received their income via a regular payroll system which included a T4 at the end of the year. It was relatively easy for the government to tax these individuals, that is to keep track of the income, and the payroll department sent tax money to the government on a monthly basis.

The trend today is toward smaller business entities, those occupying niche markets in high tech fields, and these smaller, specialized business entities employ fewer people directly. Rather, the tendency is to contract work out. The objective is to keep overhead under control and purchase skills only as needed.

Take the example of a company requiring computer programmers. Rather than employing a computer programmer on payroll, why not contract the work out to a small computer programming firm or to independent operators on a fee for service basis? It's more cost-effective and more flexible—specialists can be assigned to special projects—and "employers" don't have to worry about unemployment insurance, payroll tax, government forms, employment law and the like. (Actually, employers do have to worry about the government challenging arrangements that it believes are really employment arrangements disguised as contracting out.)

This is how the role of the Canadian employee is changing, particularly employees with specialized skills. No longer will such people have a permanent, nine-to-five job. Rather, many will become independent contractors, in the business of doing work for those who need their services on an as-needed basis, whether the government likes it or not.

As more and more of these former employees become business people servicing others, there is a change in the way they interact with Canada's income tax system. As more and more employees go into business for themselves, the collection of taxes from the traditional T4 of middle-class workers becomes less lucrative. And those in business for themselves can take advantage of certain tax planning opportunities (explained later) that are simply not open to individuals who are engaged solely as traditional employees and whose income tax is deducted at source.

I see this trend toward individual entrepreneurship and the tax planning opportunities it creates in a positive light, as part of the Great Restructuring that will enable Canadian businesses to compete globally and generate wealth in new ways, ways that will bring new prosperity in the medium to long term.

The move to a global economy has also reduced our government's ability to collect revenue in the form of corporate taxes. The large multinationals were the first to go global, as their long arms reached across national boundaries. Assume, for example, that a multinational corporation has operations in Canada and one or more jurisdictions where taxes are lower. It is obvious if you think about it that every avenue will be explored for realizing profits in the jurisdiction with the lowest tax rate. Canadian tax laws contain a number of provisions to address this type of manoeuvring, but it is extremely difficult to control.

As it now stands, since so many traditional Canadian manufacturing and resource industries are owned abroad, the Canadian government faces a dilemma. The higher Canadian corporate taxes become, the more profit will be removed from the country by transfer pricing and other means. There will also be less incentive for corporations to retain or establish branches in this country unless they are in industries that need a sophisticated work force and the kind of facilities Canada can provide.

In other words, due to the nature of our economy, the degree of foreign ownership of it and the increasing number of Canadian businesses structuring their affairs internationally from a business and tax perspective, the burden of income taxation will continue to shift increasingly to the shoulders of the individual taxpayer.

But the individual taxpayer is steadily transforming into a business person, an independent contractor without a traditional employer/employee relationship that can be taxed easily at source. That this presents a challenge to the tax collector is an understatement.

One possible solution is to abandon the income tax system and rely on consumption taxes that hit every person virtually every time goods and services are acquired. Hence the various provincial sales taxes and the Goods and Services Tax (GST).

But consumption taxes are not politically popular and are seen as regressive, hitting all Canadians equally (subject to rebates in some cases for the poorest among us) regardless of our level of income. Consumption taxes, particularly the GST, have driven more activity into the underground economy and are generally bad for consumer morale. That said, I suspect that most of us would accept the GST if the substantial revenues from it were used to retire the country's enormous debt. But that would take considerable political courage and I fear that, barring external forces such as pressure from the International Monetary Fund or the reluctance of foreign investors to buy Canada Bonds, the GST will flow into general revenues and be used by governments in traditional ways.

For these reasons, I predict that, over the next number of years, our governments will rely both on consumption taxes and income taxes. I predict increasing tax rates and a continual challenging by government of the natural progression of a significant segment of our work force from traditional employment to being in the business of generating work for themselves.

In my opinion, governments at all levels should go with the flow and stop trying to preserve an increasingly outdated notion of the Canadian status quo. Moreover, a National Business Plan is needed, one that recognizes which way the flow is going and determines how best to go with it. At present, there really is no National Business Plan, and I predict that we will see a defensive reaction to change from most governments rather than the leadership we need.

This leaves Canadians in a predicament. To provide for our long-term financial security we must free up capital and invest it wisely. But an essential element of freeing up capital is reducing the taxes we pay, and the governments of the country are shoving their hands deeper and deeper into our pockets.

It appears, therefore, that the good of the individual and the good of the state are diametrically opposed. This, in my opinion, is the classic manifestation of bad management. It is the role of a good manager, moreover, to ensure that what is good for the individual is generally good for all concerned. This is true in any organization. Imagine how poorly a corporation would be managed if what was good for the individual worker was bad for the corporation's business. In the context of a nation state, if the good of the state and the good of the individual are opposite, the ultimate result will be anarchy. Are Canadians on a collision course with government policy, particularly tax policy? This is a fundamental question.

My view of the matter is as follows. As the Great Restructuring moves Canada away from a resource-based and protectionist manufacturing economy and as individual Canadians, of necessity if not by design, become increasingly entrepreneurial, it is government policy that must change. Government must work smarter and, though it must also protect the needy among us and provide certain basic programs and encourage economic activity in which there is a good future, it must get its huge hands out of our pockets.

As governments are unlikely to do this of their own volition, and since it is essential to our long-term prosperity and financial security to invest our resources wisely, it is incumbent on all of us, particularly those in the middle to upper income range, to do two things. First, to rely on our own ingenuity and resources and stop looking to the government for help. Second, to organize our financial and business affairs to reduce the tax we pay to the lowest level reasonably allowed under Canadian tax law. It's our moral duty.

On the issue of reducing taxes, however, I would like to highlight the difference between tax avoidance and tax evasion. Tax evasion, simply put, is tax cheating: failing to declare income, lying about deductions and the like. Such behaviour is criminal in nature. Don't do it.

Tax avoidance, on the other hand, is the ordering of your business and financial affairs to reduce, in accordance with tax laws, the tax that you must pay. This is a legitimate activity, although there was a time when this fact was not settled.

A leading tax court case heard by the British Privy Council in the 1930s put the question to rest once and for all and has been cited with favour by tax courts in this country ever since. The case was the famous Duke of Westminster case heard by the Privy Council in England in 1936, wherein Lord Tomlin stated unequivocally as follows: "Every man (read "person" today) is entitled if he can to order his affairs so that the tax attaching under the appropriate acts is less than it otherwise would be. If he succeeds in ordering them so as to secure this result, then, however unappreciative the Commissioner of

Inland Revenue (read "Revenue Canada") or his fellow tax-payers may be of his ingenuity, he can not be compelled to pay an increased tax."

The Duke of Westminster decision, in short, provides that tax planning is a legal, legitimate activity. This accords, more-over, with my belief that tax planning is necessary for the long-term prosperity and financial security of the individual in particular and the nation as a whole. The quicker that governments at all levels and those Canadians who look to the government for too much realize this the quicker we will emerge from the Great Restructuring with a solid future.

Inflation

My first comment about inflation—the annual increase in the cost of basic goods and services—is that the individual investor can do nothing to prevent it or reduce it. Unlike taxes, which may be deferred or avoided to some extent through proper tax planning, inflation affects us all.

Over the past 30 years, while inflation has bounced up and down, the median rate has been approximately 4.5%. It would therefore be reasonable to assume that over the next 40 years inflation may average 4%, slightly less, and this assumption will be made throughout.

Like taxation, inflation is a powerful wealth destroyer, eroding your buying power every day. The longer it has to eat at your wealth the more damage it will do. That's another way of saying that the younger you are, the more adverse an effect inflation will have on you.

Let's take an example. Assume that you have accumulated $500,000 and that you are 40 years old. How much will

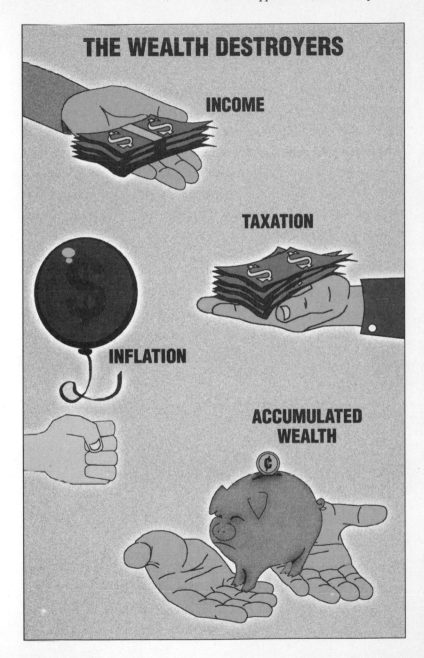

this $500,000 be worth in today's dollars—in other words discounted for inflation—when you are 65 if inflation averages 4%, as we assume? The answer is approximately $180,000, 36% as much. You will have lost 64% of your purchasing power.

What if you are 50 years old today instead of 40. How much will the $500,000 be worth when you are 65? The answer is approximately $270,000, 54% as much. You will have lost only 46% of your purchasing power because you were at war with inflation 15 years instead of 25. This is one of the few advantages of extra age in the wealth accumulation process; the older you are the less time inflation has to work its nasty business.

If you're wondering how to calculate this sort of thing for yourself, quickly and easily (and by the time you finish reading this book I think you'll want to be in a position to do that), the answer is a business/financial calculator. To assist you in this I have included in Appendix I some information on this basic wealth accumulation tool of the trade.

For present purposes, the one point you should keep in mind regarding inflation is that you must accumulate enough wealth to outrun its impact, even if you live for a very long time. The key to accomplish this lies in the magic of compound growth.

Compound Growth

How does compound growth work magic on investments? Although most Canadians will look you in the eye and insist that they understand the nature and enormous power of compound growth, it is my experience that they do not. Simply put, compound growth occurs when funds are invested so that the income earned on those funds is added to the funds, so that the income can also earn income. The effect of compound interest on wealth accumulation is tremendous and is discussed more fully below.

I must admit that I was in my mid-30s before the true power of compound growth sank in. As a professional, moreover, I began to wonder how my wife and I would be able to afford not only university educations for each of our children but be able to retire with dignity, particularly if we were blessed with considerable longevity.

My first reaction was to rush to our RRSP file to see how it was growing and to calculate how much might be there on retirement at any reasonable retirement age. Where would we be if we contributed the maximum to an RRSP each year and earned, say, 10% interest compounded annually, and if inflation were, say, 4% per year on average? How much would the after tax income be on turning 80 or 85 or even 90 years of age if I retired at 55? 60? 65?

It began to appear that we might not be able to sock away enough in an RRSP to do the job. Other investments would be required beyond the RRSP.

Additional investments. Those words cut through me like a knife. Just putting the maximum in an RRSP was a challenge in some years. Did this mean that we should go on a strict budget, a financial diet? We weren't in the habit of spending recklessly. What would we have to cut? What would our lives be like?

I made some basic calculations. Two facts were readily confirmed. First, the RRSP alone would not be enough unless it earned a consistent, substantial rate of interest and, second, if we lived too long, we would become poorer and poorer unless unrealistically high returns were achieved.

So I began working the calculations backwards, starting with an income level at age 80, 85 or 90 that would permit us to live with relative dignity at that age. My question was, how much money would we need to set aside today on a weekly, monthly or yearly basis to achieve that income level in the golden years based on a realistic rate of return? The answer literally changed our lives, including my career to some extent.

Suddenly, the light came on. It was possible to build substantial wealth, real wealth, by setting aside a relatively modest amount of money consistently and earning a decent but not outlandish rate of return. The younger one began, the more modest the amount that would be needed.

The answer was compound growth. As we've discussed, the reason compound growth has such a magic effect is that income is earned on top of income. Look at this simple example. If $100 earns 10% interest in a year, $10 is earned and the total, if the interest is not removed, becomes $110. The second year $11 is earned, being 10% of the original $100 and 10% of the $10 interest from the first year. Adding on

COMPOUNDING $100,000 AT VARIOUS RATES

Years	ANNUAL RATE OF RETURN		
	5%	10%	15%
5 years	$127,600	$161,100	$201,100
10 years	$162,900	$259,400	$404,600
15 years	$207,900	$417,700	$813,700
20 years	$265,300	$672,800	$1,636,700
25 years	$338,600	$1,083,500	$3,291,900

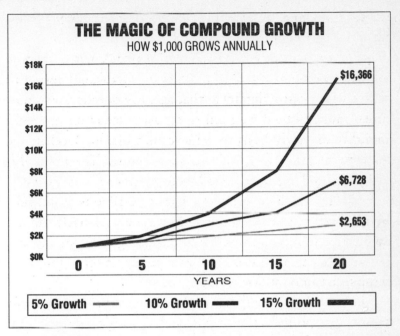

THE MAGIC OF COMPOUND GROWTH
HOW $1,000 GROWS ANNUALLY

5% Growth —— 10% Growth ▬▬ 15% Growth ▬▬▬

the $11 interest from year two, the total is now $121, $1 more than if income on income had not been earned.

Now many would say: "Big deal, $1 extra. Sure, I understand compounding." But do they understand its true significance? Do they understand the tidal wave effect it can have over time if money grows geometrically? Do they appreciate that tripling the interest rate can multiply the wealth accumulation sixfold in 20 years, tenfold in 25 years and almost one hundredfold in 50 years? Study the two tables given here to prove it to yourself if you have any doubts. Then, plan to put the principle of compound growth to work for you as you accumulate wealth for your personal financial security.

PART II

What Are You Going To Do?

4

"I Can't Build Wealth, I Don't Have Any Money"

I HEAR IT FROM CANADIANS IN ALL WALKS OF LIFE. I hear it from individuals on middle and upper incomes. I hear it from executives, independent business people and professionals like dentists and physicians. Yes, I hear it from all over, from places you would expect to hear it and places you would not.

What I hear is that none of these individuals can afford to build wealth; they can't get started because all of their earnings are already spoken for. Right now they are too cash poor to begin a program of wealth accumulation.

The first step in the wealth building program must be to break out of this "too cash poor to get started" state by taking steps to free up some capital. Without capital it's generally not possible to accumulate wealth. It's tough to build something out of nothing.

FINDING MONEY TO INVEST

What you must do is set aside a fixed amount—$50 a week or $100 a week—or whatever amount is required to achieve your financial objectives. The younger you start the more you can accumulate and the sooner you can achieve the desired level of financial security. Alternatively, the younger you start, the smaller the weekly amount of money you'll need to set aside.

It's my preference to set money aside weekly rather than monthly because for me, it's easier to put smaller amounts aside more frequently. But how much money should you put aside each week? How much money are you going to need? Assuming that income taxes can be deferred through tax sheltering and assuming a steady rate of inflation, the variables that must be analysed to answer this question are as follows:

- your age when you begin;
- the age when you plan to retire;
- the average interest or growth rate you achieve.

Let's take an example. Assume you start somewhere between 20 and 50 years of age. Assume you want to retire at 65. Assume an average annual rate of return of 18%, 15%, 12% or 9%. Assume that your long-term objective is to accumulate, just by way of example, $1,000,000 in today's dollars, with today's buying power. Using my financial calculator I have determined that, to have the equivalent of $1,000,000 at the age of 65, if you're a 20 year old and the average annual inflation rate is 4%, you would have to accumulate $5,841,175.70. In other words, 45 years from now (when you would turn 65) $5,841,175.70 would be worth $1,000,000 in today's dollars because of inflation.

Making the same type of calculation for each age group (in five year intervals) we can produce the following figures.

AGE	AMOUNT TO ACCUMULATE
20	$5,841,175.70
25	$4,801,020.60
30	$3,946,089.00
35	$3,243,397.50
40	$2,665,836.30
45	$2,191,123.10
50	$1,800,843.50

The effect of 4% annual inflation has a significant impact on the amount of money you must accumulate, although the impact is less significant the older you are when you start accumulating because inflation has less time to erode your wealth.

But the younger you begin, the more time you have to take advantage of compound interest. Assume, therefore, an annual rate of return of 18%, 15%, 12% or 9% (the higher the rate of return the better, obviously) and study the following example. From this example, you will be able to determine how much money you would have to invest *weekly* to achieve the targets set out above.

WEEKLY INVESTMENTS AT VARIOUS ANNUAL RATES OF RETURN				
AGE	18%	15%	12%	9%
20	$ 6.23	$ 19.95	$ 61.54	$ 179.90
25	12.57	34.71	92.45	234.17
30	25.40	60.51	139.32	306.64
35	51.42	105.79	211.16	405.46
40	104.48	186.23	323.51	544.79
45	214.43	332.68	506.01	752.41
50	451.40	614.28	825.08	1,092.57

It's clear from this table that the younger you start, the more you can accumulate or the sooner you can retire, but now that it's clear that results can be significant, where are you going to find that weekly amount of money you want to set aside?

Budgets

First, a few comments about setting up and living on a budget. At the level of the individual household, I am not a great fan of budgets. They have an important place in business but there are few individuals who have the discipline necessary to make them work at the household level.

Budgets are fiscal diets and like the other kind of diet, they work for a while and then we tend to wander. In other words, they generally don't work. It's important to keep your expenses under control because money spent cannot be invested. But the key to success here is to find places where money is currently being spent unnecessarily and to reallocate those monies to investment instead.

Budgets work on the principle that you should spend a certain amount on accommodation, transportation, food and so forth and save the funds left over. In theory this is a very sensible approach; in practice it doesn't work for most people, probably because of the discipline required to make sure something is left over and the fact that the imposition of that discipline makes the exercise feel like a continuing sacrifice. You end up counting nickels and dimes the way dieters count calories and the budget, like a strict diet, is on your mind all the time. It affects every decision every day and casts a shadow over your lifestyle. Cash reallocation is fundamentally different because it involves a fairly simple decision that should not go on to haunt your day-to-day existence.

I know from working with middle and upper income Canadians that they are generally not willing to sacrifice lifestyle or live with constant reminders of limitations on their freedom to do as they wish. I understand this, although it's alarming to see the extent to which a middle or upper income Canadian can spend literally every cent that comes in the door no matter how large the net income.

Put another way, we can steal an axiom from management theory and say that the cost of living expands to fill the income available. There is virtually no limit to the amount of money that can slip through your fingers if you make no plan to control it. Certainly a budget would work wonders, *if* it worked.

I have read many dozens of books over the years on financial planning. It has become apparent to me that those that insist on disciplined budgeting generally miss the mark.

Rather, it is books such as David Chilton's *The Wealthy Barber* that get it right. The key to saving money is to pay yourself first, take a certain amount off the top of every dollar that comes into the household and use that for investment. The balance of the money is your disposable income and can be spent however you wish. A budget becomes unnecessary since you will then live automatically within your means.

The principle of paying yourself first came home in real terms to me during the years I spent as a salaried employee; I was a tax lawyer with the Government of Canada some time back. I noticed, or rather my wife noticed, that my annual raise didn't seem to have any obvious effect on our standard of living. The extra money just seemed to disappear.

The fact that a middle to upper income earner can have an increase in gross income of 5% or 10% or more and not necessarily experience an appreciable difference in standard of living leads to an interesting question. Is it possible to decrease your net income and not experience an appreciable reduction in living standards? The answer for most of us is yes. And the higher your net income, the truer this is.

Setting Money Aside

Assume a net income, for example, of $4,000 a month (or $10,000 a month in Harry and Dolly's case). Would it make an appreciable difference to your standard of living if this net income were reduced by 10% to $3,600 (or $9,000) a month? The answer for most is no.

What if this 10% reduction were taken right off the top by automatic bank transfer or similar means and invested wisely? Would not significant wealth be created over time? Go back to the charts on pages 57 and 58 to see the returns on $105 a week invested at 15% from age 35. The answer is yes.

This concept of paying yourself first has been referred to in a number of publications, including *The Wealthy Barber*, as the "10% solution." I believe in it. It works, particularly when combined with a good average annual rate of return and the added bonus of tax sheltering strategies.

I have a few refinements to the 10% solution that I would like to add. First, as you move up the income scale and more disposable income is available, I would suggest that you increase the 10% solution to the 11%, 12%, 13%, 14% or 15% solution. Harry and Dolly with their $10,000 a month disposable income, for example, would still have $8,500 a month available if 15% ($1,500) were set aside monthly. They could still go out for dinner to relax and the money could be spent without any feeling of being cramped by the discipline of a budget. And their funds set aside for investment would not be sitting in their chequing account, begging to be spent. So do not assume that 10% is the upper limit. Neither does it have to be the lower limit. Treat it merely as a guideline.

But those on higher incomes already set aside, or should set aside, the maximum in RRSP contributions (18% of earned income, 9% after tax for those in the highest tax bracket and 11% for those in the middle bracket). Should this be considered part of the 10% solution? My answer is a qualified no. In the first instance, the government in effect is paying a significant portion of the contribution to the RRSP. Second, we have determined that contributing to an RRSP alone may not be enough to provide fully for retirement. More is needed, especially for those over 40.

But what if you are just starting out, just beginning to put the maximum into an RRSP? My advice is to put a few percentage points above your allowable RRSP contribution away, as much as possible. Invest in your future, even if the extra investment is not tax deductible. The younger you are the lower the percentage can be because you'll have more time for the tax sheltered compounding inside the RRSP to work in your favour. Try 3% or 5% and sneak it up to 10% over time as your income increases and the number of working years to retirement decreases. And I strongly recommend making the maximum RRSP contributions at the beginning of each year or at least monthly.

Further, since Canadian law limits RRSP contributions to 18% of earned income to an eventual annual maximum contribution limit of $15,500 (indexed after it reaches that limit), it is particularly important for those whose earned income precludes contributing to the maximum limit to use additional means such as the 10% solution. This ceiling on RRSP contributions probably means your accumulated funds won't be enough unless you build other investments. The same is generally true for many on company pension plans. Additional resources will be needed to build the long-term financial security you will want to have. Even for those of you at the highest earned income levels, some variation of the 10% solution—paying yourself first—should be a part of your wealth accumulation program, in addition to making the maximum allowable RRSP contributions.

But, as I said at the outset, the answer I get from middle income earners, upper income earners, dentists, physicians, other professionals and business people across the land is:

"You must be kidding. I can barely afford to make my RRSP contributions. Where will the money come from?"

The first and simplest answer is just do it: put in place a weekly regime that removes from your grasp enough to make your RRSP contributions and 10% more (plus or minus). Not only will you manage on the remainder, but you likely won't notice any material difference in your standard of living.

The more sophisticated answer builds on this idea. While it is true that if you have less money to waste, you will waste less money, it is also true that it is possible to organize your affairs to cut out particular pockets of waste and unnecessary expenditures right at the beginning. This is not by way of a budget, but a methodical review of your affairs to determine where real waste is occurring. Are you paying interest charges on credit cards because you aren't paying off the balance in time? Clear the amount owing. Are you shopping on impulse or using shopping as a recreation? Find something else to do with your time. Are you paying membership dues, subscription fees and other regular expenses for goods and services you never use? Go through your chequebook and find out where your money is going. I guarantee you will find money that would be better used for investment.

Personal Debt

Take a close look at your overall debt load. In addition to paying off your credit cards, gradually pay off your mortgage. In fact, pay off all debt over time, particularly debt that is not tax deductible, generally that debt borrowed for personal rather than business purposes. All such non-deductible debt is payable in after tax dollars and is very expensive indeed.

You may want to go so far as to establish a program or strategy to reduce debt, including the home mortgage, by making additional payments should your contracts with lenders so permit. Take all steps reasonably possible to reduce your debt load in whatever manner may be available to you.

Why is debt such a wealth destroyer? Assume, as an example, that you have a loan or mortgage at an interest rate of 9% per annum and assume it is not tax deductible. If you're in the 50% tax bracket, you'd have to earn 18% per annum in pretax dollars from an investment to be as well off as if you used your resources to pay off the loan or mortgage. The reason is that the loan or mortgage payment must be made with after tax dollars and it is difficult enough to earn twice the cost of the borrowed funds consistently without taking undue risk. The low risk strategy (really a no-risk strategy) is to retire such debt as soon as possible.

So where will the money to accomplish this come from? If I reduce debt before I begin investing, will I ever be in a position to begin? One approach is to take half of your 10% solution for this purpose. If you are setting aside 8%, for example, use 4% to retire non-deductible debt and invest the other 4%. This way you are reducing your debt load and gaining experience at investing while enjoying the positive feeling that comes from knowing that wealth is accumulating even as you sleep.

The next advice is to avoid investing overly in depreciables. Depreciables are assets, such as cars, stereos and the like, that generally go down in value year after year. It's not possible to make money buying things that go down in value. Look around your home and use your calculator to add up the replacement value of all your depreciables. For a typical middle or upper income Canadian household, this replacement value would be somewhere between $20,000 and $100,000 or more, with $50,000 perhaps being the average. If you compute the future value 20 years down the road of the $50,000 tied up in these depreciables, you'll discover that 20 years from now the money "invested" in these depreciables, had it been invested in growth assets, would have had a value at 12% growth (not discounted for inflation) of $482,314.65.

Now, I understand that certain depreciables are necessary and that certain others are the kinds of things that middle and upper income Canadians aren't prepared to do without. The car, snowblower, lawn mower and the like are a must for many Canadians. A television set (or two) is something else that most middle and upper income Canadians would not be willing to forgo.

But be smart. Don't invest too heavily in depreciables. With respect to the car, common wisdom has it that buying a slightly used model, typically one about two years old, will put you behind the wheel of something you would be proud to drive and with lots of good life left. It's during the first two years of ownership that the real bang of depreciation hits a car owner. Just be prudent with depreciables, that's all, because there is wealth to build. The difference can be dramatic.

Tax Planning

Tax planning is another way to free up cash for investment but it raises the spectre of accountants, meetings and complicated forms. This makes many taxpayers reluctant to try it. But it's worth pointing out that those in the middle and upper income brackets sometimes spend more on taxes in a year than on anything else. In fact, it's not uncommon for an upper income Canadian to spend more on income tax than on accommodation and transportation combined. Look at the amount you paid in taxes last year and compare it with your other major expenses. Wouldn't you prefer to use some of this money for your own investments rather than handing it over to the government?

Tax planning is a must if you want to cut down your contribution to government coffers. It's amazing what a small percentage of Canadians actually do any tax planning. We all know that taxes are one of the "inevitables" in life, but what many of us don't realize is that the amount of tax we pay is not preordained. And sometimes the savings generated from effective tax planning can fund your entire wealth accumulation program. That's why tax planning is such an important part of any strategy to free up cash for investment.

Tax planning consists, in its simplest terms, of organizing your affairs within the rules of Canadian tax law to minimize the income tax that you pay.

There are two basic aspects to tax planning: saving taxes today and deferring taxes to tomorrow. Both are important tools in the wealth accumulation arsenal.

Tax Savings   Tax savings are generated by reducing taxable income. Taxable income can be reduced by decreasing gross income or increasing allowable deductions from gross income.

While reducing gross income may be accomplished simply by earning less, earning a dollar less to save a half a dollar in tax is not going to help you get ahead. The trick is to earn the same dollar but reduce the tax bite from 50% to, say, 25%.

One way to save taxes is to increase allowable deductions. This is best accomplished with the help of a knowledgeable and reasonably aggressive tax accountant. Hiring shrewd advice is the best way to ensure that valuable deductions aren't missed and that you understand how to keep all receipts and other records necessary to validate your claim to those deductions.

One of the more popular but ultimately self-defeating ways to increase deductions is to lose money in a bad business venture. If you lose enough money and thereby claim enough losses, certainly there will be little or no tax to pay. But again, this is not the kind of tax saving that will enable you to accumulate wealth. Losing a dollar to save half a dollar is the route to financial failure. I see this technique used all too often by professionals—dentists and physicians take the cake—particularly when they are buying "tax shelters."

There are a number of books on how to increase deductions legitimately, covering a myriad of points from the very small to the reasonably large. These tactics should be employed aggressively but there is a limit to what can be accomplished by increasing deductions. No, the real key is to structure your affairs to reduce taxes as a direct result of that structuring and to invest the tax savings in your future.

Tax Deferral   This basic tax device is an important part of any wealth accumulation strategy. It consists of postponing the tax that you would otherwise pay until a later date. One important tax deferral strategy is to place money in a tax sheltered vehicle to permit compound growth without paying tax immediately on the income generated.

As an example, if you contribute to a Registered Retirement Savings Plan (RRSP) and buy an investment with that money—perhaps a Guaranteed Investment Certificate (GIC)—that investment will generate interest income that will not be taxed as it is earned from year to year. Instead, the interest income will be sheltered from all income taxes as long as the money stays inside the RRSP. The money will compound tax free and will only be taxed when it is removed from the RRSP. Funds earning income in such a sheltered environment will grow dramatically because there is that much more money (the money that would have gone in taxes) to generate more income. But, you ask, what good is all that money locked up in an RRSP? Isn't the income fully taxable when the money is taken out? Won't I lose so much of that compounded income that the benefit of the investment will be lost?

Let's compare the same amount of money, invested at the same rate of interest for the same amount of time, in both a sheltered and fully taxable environment. Assume that $10,000 is invested in an RRSP. Assume an annual rate of interest of 12%. Money invested at 12% will, in the absence of income tax, double approximately every 6 years. This fact can be confirmed by using the "Rule of 72s": divide the number 72 by the after tax interest rate (in this case $72 \div 12\% = 6$) to determine the number of years it will take money to double. The Rule of 72s is a handy way to make quick (but approximate) calculations.

At a marginal tax rate of 50% it is true that if the money is withdrawn at the end of the investment period, half of it will go in taxes. But it is also true that if the same money is invested in a taxable environment, the 50% marginal tax rate will cut the income accumulated to 6% per year as the other half goes in annual taxes. The real interest rate for the taxable investment is now 6% and it will take approximately twice as long for this money to double (72 ÷ by 6% = 12 years).

As you can see in the table below, your $10,000 investment can, after 36 years, net you $640,000 in before tax return on investment ($320,000 after the tax to be paid on withdrawal from the tax sheltered environment) or $80,000 in the non-sheltered environment (where the tax has been paid annually as returns on investment were earned). The choice is yours. Let no one tell you that tax deferral in the form of tax sheltered growth is not a powerful wealth accumulation strategy.

TAX SHELTERED INVESTMENT		INVESTMENT TAXABLE ANNUALLY
$ 10,000.00	Year 0	$10,000.00
$ 20,000.00	Year 6	
$ 40,000.00	Year 12	$20,000.00
$ 80,000.00	Year 18	
$160,000.00	Year 24	$40,000.00
$320,000.00	Year 30	
$640,000.00	Year 36	$80,000.00

Tax Shelters Because I believe so strongly in tax sheltering, I would like to distinguish between a so-called "tax shelter" and "tax sheltering." The term "tax shelter" is generally applied to certain investments that are structured according to tax law to enable the investor to receive an immediate deduction and participate in the risk of the business venture over the years ahead. An example would be limited partnerships to fund resource exploration or other activities the government wishes to encourage from time to time by offering tax breaks to encourage money to flow into those sectors.

Tax shelters are particularly attractive to professionals with high incomes because they provide immediate tax savings. But the savings come with the underlying business risks involved in the particular venture. Sometimes these risks will be extremely high. Sometimes the potential profit from the venture has been stripped away by the promoters of the venture by excessive management fees.

That is not to say that all tax shelters are bad. On the contrary, some are good and offer significant opportunities for tax saving. The challenge is to distinguish good from bad, and this is not necessarily an easy thing to do. For this reason, I generally avoid tax shelters.

Rather than use the term "tax shelter," therefore, I prefer the terms "tax sheltering" or "tax sheltered," which may be defined as placing funds in a vehicle, such as an RRSP, where the growth is sheltered from income tax until it is withdrawn, providing an opportunity for tax sheltered growth—in other words, tax deferral.

TAX PLANNING STRATEGIES

For those on middle and upper incomes, there are several basic tax planning strategies that may be used to reduce the effect of income tax on wealth accumulation, thereby freeing up cash for investment. Actually, there are dozens of techniques of varying significance, most well canvassed in a plethora of books available at Canadian bookstores.

My approach, however, is to treat reducing taxes as but the first step in a wealth accumulation program. It's not enough to save taxes or, for that matter, to defer taxes. After all, our objective is to achieve wealth. Since many Canadians are in a position to do that but don't, I am explaining the framework that will enable you to approach this challenge and showing you just what is possible. Therefore, the following is an overview of the major tools that may be utilized by many on middle and upper incomes to lower taxes today and defer taxes to tomorrow.

First, it is necessary to distinguish between traditional employees on T4s and the existing and emerging group of individuals in the business of providing their services to others, the independent contractors. There is generally less room for tax planning for those in an employer/employee relationship on a traditional T4. That is by no means the end of the story, however. Some of the following tax planning strategies will be as appropriate for traditional employees as for non-traditional ones and this will be highlighted throughout as applicable.

The RRSP

One of the best aspects of the RRSP is that tax saving and tax deferral overlap and work together. First, you get an immediate deduction for the allowable contribution made to the RRSP. This results in a lowering of taxable income and therefore a tax saving today. Then, the monies placed in the RRSP grow in a tax sheltered environment. This facilitates compound growth for wealth accumulation and is classic tax deferral. And to close the circle, the tax saving can become part of the next year's contribution to the RRSP. For these reasons, the

RRSP is a particularly powerful tax planning device. It's a shame that more Canadians do not use it and use it wisely.

Corporations

The Small Business   The income tax treatment of corporations is quite different from the income tax treatment of individuals. First, the tax rate. While corporations in Canada are generally subject to a tax of approximately 44%, there is a deduction for certain small businesses that effectively lowers the tax rate to approximately 22% on the first $200,000 of active business income. Although these tax rates vary according to province and type of business activity, for simplicity in our examples, we will assume corporate tax rates of 44% and, where the small business deduction applies, 22%.

Many individuals look at this lower corporate tax rate (22%) with envy and give thought to incorporating their business activities to take advantage of it. From a wealth accumulation perspective, this tax rate, where it can be achieved, can have a positive impact on the amount of wealth that can be accumulated.

So just who can form a corporation to do business? The simple answer is that most adults or groups of adults can, but certain professionals in certain provinces are not permitted to incorporate their professional activities as we have noted. For most of us however, instead of pursuing business activities as a sole proprietor (an unincorporated individual in business) or a partnership (two or more individuals in business together), it is generally possible to form a corporation to pursue those business activities.

When you pursue business as a sole proprietor, you do so as an individual, even if you register a business name with the government for carrying on your business. You will also be taxed on your profits (income less expenses) at individual income tax rates.

A partnership is a bit more complicated. In a partnership, two or more individuals pursue business together, jointly and severally responsible—as the legal saying goes—for each other's actions in the common purpose (including business debts and other partnership liabilities). In other words, the partnership liabilities of one partner are the liability of all, and vice versa. Profit is calculated at the partnership level (partnership income less partnership expenses) but the profit is not taxed there. Rather, it is flowed out to the partners according to their respective ownership of the partnership (or such other basis as the partners may choose) and taxed in their hands as individuals at individual income tax rates.

Either way—sole proprietor or partnership—you will pay income tax on profits at individual tax rates according to the usual individual income tax brackets. But a corporation is a separate legal entity, a separate legal creature, with a business and tax life of its own. Unlike an individual, whether that individual is a sole practitioner or partner, a corporation is subject to corporate tax laws, a different kettle of fish from individual tax laws as you will see, and this is where you may be able to take advantage of a lower tax rate.

Now, let's take this example. Assume that you earn $25,000 a year and that this $25,000 is earned from a consulting business perhaps run on nights and weekends and is in addition to your nine-to-five job.

Assume that this business on the side is not incorporated. In other words, you carry on the business as a sole proprietor. Let's compare the tax treatment of that income with the same income in an incorporated business—a corporation that has been formed complete with articles of incorporation, directors and shareholders.

Assume that the cost of running this small consulting business, no matter what its legal status, is $5,000 a year, including the cost of running a home office, supplies, marketing, travel and the like. Assuming no other subtleties of accounting or tax law, the profit would therefore be $20,000.

If this small consulting business were incorporated and qualified for the small business deduction and the 22% tax rate on the first $200,000, the taxes to be paid by such a small incorporated business would be $4,400 ($20,000 x 22%). Were the business not incorporated, the tax payable for an individual in the top tax bracket would be $10,000 ($20,000 x 50%).

It would appear on the surface at least that taxes could be cut by more than half and $5,600 a year could be saved, more in those provinces where the highest marginal tax rate for individuals is above 50%. Note that this result would apply both to traditional employees (subject to restrictions with respect to personal services businesses, discussed below) and to independent contractors, either of whom are entitled to have a corporation to do business, on the side after hours, provided that as a traditional employee, the terms of employment don't prohibit you from doing this.

While incorporating this business will be quite attractive from the standpoint of tax savings, it's important to note that the Income Tax Act places restrictions on the use of the small business deduction.

1. The corporation must be a Canadian-controlled Private Corporation (CCPC), which means that it must not be controlled directly or indirectly by one or more non-resident persons or public corporations. This is generally not a problem, although it is an absolute requirement.

2. The deduction applies only to that portion of the CCPC's income that qualifies as "active" business income rather than "passive." Active business income is defined for these purposes as income from any business carried on by the CCPC other than a specified investment business or a personal services business.

A "specified investment business" is defined as a business the principal purpose of which is to derive income from property (including interest, dividends, rents or royalties) unless the corporation employs more than five full-time employees throughout the year. In other words, you cannot isolate your investments in a corporation to earn interest, dividends, rents or royalties or other income from property and have that income taxed at the small business rate.

A "personal services business" is defined as the business of providing services where the individual (or any person related to that individual) who performs services for the corporation is a shareholder who could reasonably be regarded as an "incorporated employee." An incorporated employee is an individual who would reasonably be regarded as an employee of the person (the employer) to which the services are provided but for the fact that the corporation had been incorporated, again unless the corporation employs more than five full-time employees throughout the year. In other words, individuals who may reasonably be considered to be employees can't incorporate and thus have their employment income taxed at the corporate small business rate instead of the higher personal rate. There must really be an active business venture.

It is even more important to note that, even where the small business deduction applies, additional tax will be levied on income removed from the corporation in the form of salaries or dividends. In fact, the rules have been crafted in such a fashion that there will generally be little or no overall advantage to incorporation unless the income is left inside the corporation.

Such income could be left inside the corporation and invested in active business activities so that the corporation's status as an active small business would not be affected. But if income is left inside the corporation and invested in property such as interest bearing instruments, stocks and the like, eventually Revenue Canada may argue that the principal purpose of the business is one of earning income from property, that the principal purpose is not to have an active business but rather to invest passively. The small business deduction could then be lost. Professional tax planning advice is advisable in this area.

Next is the issue of losses. Generally, when one establishes a new business it will incur losses at the outset rather than make a profit. If a corporation suffers a loss, say, in the first year of operations it can set those losses aside on paper and use them in a later year or years. Corporate losses, in fact, may be carried forward and applied to any of the next seven taxation years. For a corporation, losses may also be carried back and applied to any of the preceding three taxation years.

But if the consulting business in question were not to be incorporated right at the outset, in other words if you were to carry on the business initially as a sole proprietor, these business losses may be written off against other income, for example against employment income, thereby reducing individual tax payable.

Would it not be better, therefore, if a loss is anticipated during those months or years necessary to get the business up and rolling profitably, not to incorporate at first? The answer may indeed be yes, subject to the qualification that there are certain other advantages to being incorporated, not the least of which is the degree of limited liability that comes from doing business in a corporate form rather than in your own name. This point should be discussed with legal counsel when deciding whether to incorporate.

From a tax perspective, it is generally advantageous to postpone incorporation where initial losses are anticipated and to write these losses off against other income, including employment income. You can incorporate at a later time, when the business turns profitable. If you are an employee on a T4, these losses could have the effect of generating a tax refund and in any event could have the effect of reducing personal income tax otherwise payable. If you are in the 50% tax bracket, your tax saving could be 50 cents of every dollar of the loss incurred from the additional, unincorporated business venture. A $10,000 loss could therefore result in a $5,000 reduction in personal taxes payable. This loss is more beneficial to the individual taxpayer than it would be locked away in a small business corporation with a much lower tax rate.

What is to stop you, therefore, from starting a business, incurring losses, and writing those losses off against other income to reduce taxes year after year? First, as noted above, losing money continually, while it may reduce taxes, is not the way to accumulate wealth. Second, there is the "business purpose test." Canadian tax law requires that you have a reasonable expectation of profit from a business venture.

But all of that said, there is no doubt that having a small business on the side can have certain tax advantages and earn you extra money for your wealth accumulation program while at the same time making a positive impact on the level of economic activity in the country. And should you incorporate your business venture, it can provide additional tax savings in the circumstances we have discussed. And there can be additional benefits to having a corporation for married Canadians and those with children.

Income Splitting

Income splitting is the tax planning technique whereby your affairs are organized to divide income among yourself and your spouse and children.

Assuming that a spouse or child is in a lower tax bracket, it may be possible to place some of the profits from a business venture in their hands by paying them a salary or by having them purchase shares in your corporation and paying them dividends.

Please note that Revenue Canada will require that salaries paid to spouses and children be reasonable in the circumstances and genuinely in return for services rendered to the business venture. Note also that Revenue Canada has an aversion to the technique of simply setting up a corporation and splitting the shares among family members in lower tax brackets. Careful tax planning is required here. Do not proceed without professional tax advice.

But that said, income splitting with family members in lower tax brackets will save tax. How much tax? The answer is directly related to the amount of income you split and the differential in the tax brackets. For example, if you split $20,000 in income with family members who are in the 25% tax bracket when you would have paid 50% tax on that income, the tax saving would be $5,000 ($20,000 x 50% − $20,000 x 25%), a sizeable tax saving. By using a corporation and something called the dividend tax credit, it may be possible in certain circumstances to do even better than that. This possibility is included below in the discussion of children's trusts.

Children's Trusts

An interesting and potentially powerful tool that may be used with or without a corporation, particularly by those with significant assets or good revenue streams, is the children's trust.

The common law definition of a trust is a right or confidence in one or more persons, called the trustee, for the benefit of one or more other persons, commonly called the beneficiaries, with respect to property. The property, whether real estate or personal property, is held in trust by the trustee for the benefit of the beneficiaries.

This is not intended to be a course in the law of trusts or a guide to setting up or using a children's trust. Rather, these comments are by way of introduction to the tax and wealth accumulation aspects of the children's trust vehicle for those readers with children. Obviously, professional advice is necessary to establish a trust of this nature. Readers to whom the civil law of Quebec applies should note that the concepts described here are different in that jurisdiction and, again, professional advice is necessary.

In the family context, most often the parents act as trustees for one or more children, the beneficiaries. Generally, there are three trustees, the parents and one other person. The trust is established and the rules for it set out in a trust settlement, a long document generally prepared by a lawyer familiar with the law of trusts.

More particularly, it is the trustees who administer and run the trust but it's another individual, called a settlor—often a close family member such as a grandparent or, where only one parent acts as trustee, the other parent—who actually establishes or creates the trust at the outset and places the initial property in it. In practice, the settlor would make an irrevocable transfer of property, generally a sum of money, to the trust to be held in trust by the trustees for the beneficiaries subject to the terms set out in the trust settlement.

Virtually any type of property can be placed in trust, including money, investments, real estate and valuables. It should be pointed out that once property is placed in the trust it cannot be removed or returned to the person who put it there. Rather, the property will be held in trust by the trustees and either accumulated for the benefit of the beneficiaries or flowed directly out to one or more of them.

A well crafted trust settlement often provides that, while the property in the trust ultimately belongs to the beneficiaries and the trustees have a duty to look after the property in the best interests of the beneficiaries, the trustees have many wide-sweeping powers to look after the trust property, including the power to invest the trust property or to distribute it to one or more of the beneficiaries whenever the trustees so decide.

The trustees generally have the right to distribute the property, in their sole discretion, evenly or unevenly to the beneficiaries. Even in the case of a single beneficiary, the trustees generally have the power to distribute property or spend money from the trust on behalf of the beneficiary at any time before the trust is wound up, provided that such money is spent for the beneficiary's benefit.

As a matter of practice, children's trusts may be established for any child under the age of majority. The trust, however, may run into adulthood, for example to the age of 25 years, as a further instrument of control. The original trust settlement generally provides for a time when the trust will be wound up and the property distributed to the beneficiaries according to its terms. Frequently, parents will also instruct the lawyer preparing the trust to have it come to an end and the property distributed on the death of the surviving parent.

In its simplest terms, therefore, a children's trust is a vehicle that enables parents to place property in children's hands irrevocably but enables the parents to control the use of that property until such time as the trust is wound up, provided that the property is used for the children's benefit and not for some other purpose. In addition, monies may be accumulated in the children's trust to provide for educational, medical and any other needs of one or more of the beneficiaries.

Tens of thousands of Canadians, traditionally the wealthier among us, use children's trusts as vehicles in the tax planning and wealth building process. In my view, the use of children's trusts should and inevitably will become more widespread. Permit me to explain.

First, a children's trust is, from a tax perspective, treated as if it were an individual, fully taxable but without the tax credits and the like that individual taxpayers get. In other words, if property were placed in the trust and that property earned income and that income were not flowed out to the beneficiaries, the children's trust would be fully taxable on that income, at the top marginal rate for an individual.

There is a rule in the Income Tax Act, however, that permits a choice (called an election) to be made to treat income accumulated in a trust as if it had in fact been flowed out to the beneficiaries. This election is called the preferred beneficiary election. Those planning to accumulate income of this sort in a children's trust would generally make the preferred beneficiary election.

When the preferred beneficiary election is made, the income will be treated as if it were in the beneficiaries' hands and will be taxed in their hands accordingly. In the case of children with little or no other income, a certain amount could be dealt with in this way without tax consequences. In this situation, the children would have too little income to attract income tax and the trust would be considered not to have taxable income as a result of the election.

But enter the Attribution Rules. Under the Income Tax Act there are a number of rules that restrict the ability to split income with family members and these affect trusts. These are called the Attribution Rules. If parents were to make a gift of money, for example, to a children's trust so that it could earn income for the benefit of the children, the Attribution Rules provide that, whether the preferred beneficiary election is made or not, the income will be taxed back in the parents' hands as if the gift had never been made. The same rules apply with respect to money loaned rather than given to a children's trust.

At the present time, however, the Income Tax Act does not attribute back to a parent giving or lending to the benefit of children any capital gains that may arise. Briefly, capital gains arise when you sell a capital property (land, stocks, etc.) for more than its adjusted cost base (basically, its cost). Ignoring the niceties, if you buy a stock, shares in a mutual fund, a piece of real estate or other capital property at a certain price and sell it at a higher price (subject to certain adjustments that need not be explored for present purposes and ignoring that land may be a capital or non-capital property) the profit on the sale may be a capital gain rather than business income.

Assuming that we are dealing with a capital gain, it is significant that a gift or loan to a children's trust will not trigger attribution back to the parents for any capital gains earned inside the trust. In other words, if parents were to give or lend money to a children's trust and buy shares, say, in a mutual fund with those monies, any capital gain realized from the sale of those shares would not be taxed in the parents' hands.

If the capital gains were flowed out to the children or if the preferred beneficiary election were made and if the amount of capital gains did not have the effect of bringing the children's income up to the level where it would attract income tax, no income tax at all would be paid on those capital gains.

Subject to the capital gains exemption (discussed below), if the amount of capital gains were sufficiently high to bring the children into the taxable range, the first dollars of such income would be taxed at the lowest marginal tax rate rather than at a higher rate. This is classic income splitting and, although it can be accomplished without a children's trust per se, the combined effect of the flexibility and powers of such a trust on the one hand and the ability to avoid attribution on capital gains on the other makes the children's trust a powerful tax and financial planning tool. Furthermore, income on income (growth compounded on top of growth) is similarly not subject at present to income attribution back to the parents, whether in the form of capital gains or not.

But the children's trust has even greater potential for dividend income from the shares of a corporation of the type discussed above. If you or your spouse, or both, were to incorporate your main business activities or a side business, it might be possible to have the children's trust acquire a portion of the shares in your corporation and thereby be in a position to receive dividend income. Dividend income under present tax laws receives favourable treatment by virtue of a mechanism known as the dividend tax credit. At the risk of oversimplifying, where the beneficiary of a trust is a child without income from other sources, the first $23,000 (approximately) of annual dividend income would not be taxed in the child's hands by virtue of the dividend tax credit. Note that the dividend tax credit is not limited to children or children's trusts. Spouses and other individuals can benefit from it, too. The discussion of this tax credit is limited here, for convenience, to the context of children's trusts.

Let's take an example. Assume that you have incorporated an active family business and that one-third of the shares were owned by you, one-third by your spouse and one-third by a children's trust in favour of your two children. Assume the after tax net income of the corporation to be $132,000 in a given year.

Assume all the $132,000 to be paid out equally in dividends, in other words, $44,000 to you, $44,000 to your spouse and $44,000 to the children's trust. The first point to note is that the $88,000 being paid out to you and your spouse is being split equally between you, thereby not pushing either of you into the highest tax bracket on this account alone, ignoring for this discussion the specifics of the rules relating to dividend income and the so-called "gross up" mechanism.

But also note that the $44,000 going to the children's trust could be divided equally between your two children. Each child would therefore receive $22,000. Both children would be eligible for the dividend tax credit and would therefore be entitled to receive the $22,000 in dividends without additional tax consequences, assuming that your children had no other source of income.

Remember that the corporation will have paid the corporate rate of tax, which (as discussed under the previous heading) we will presume to be approximately 22%. The fact that one-third of the corporation's income could be distributed without further tax consequences will generate an obvious overall tax saving.

But would you want to place $22,000 in the hands of a child? The answer in most circumstances would be no, and in that case the choices are twofold. First, you could use the preferred beneficiary election and keep the money in the trust to accumulate for a rainy day. Second, the funds could be spent by you throughout the year for the child's benefit to the extent that there are legitimate reasons to spend the funds on the child. Further, it is possible to combine these two alternatives.

Let me explain. It is most common that the parents would have the children's trust open a children's trust bank account with chequing privileges. The parents would then carry with them a children's trust chequebook and write cheques on monies in the children's trust account according to the children's needs. The rule to watch here is that the money genuinely be spent for the children's needs and not for the needs of the parents. It would be open to the child later in life to sue the parents if the parents spent trust monies on the parents' needs. The parents have a duty in their capacity as trustees to act in the best interest of the children as beneficiaries. Furthermore, Revenue Canada would take a dim view of the entire arrangement if the parents were to breach their duty as trustees in this manner.

It is common in the context of a children's trust for parents to buy things for the children as needed by writing cheques on the children's trust bank account. Cheques could be written for clothing, summer camp, piano lessons, private school tuition and the like. In this way, overall household expenses are reduced and the income of the trust is being used in favour of the beneficiaries who are either not taxable at all or who may be taxable in a lower tax bracket. Yet control remains in the hands of the parents.

Note once again that Revenue Canada has a general aversion to income splitting and that it is important, therefore, to structure the children's trust and any monies given, loaned or declared by dividends to it in a manner that will generally accord with tax law and Revenue Canada's policies. Professional assistance should be sought.

There is no doubt that children's trusts are a potent device for tax planning and for building wealth. From a wealth accumulation perspective, it is possible to envisage a children's trust being used to accumulate significant amounts of wealth for the benefit of the children.

CAPITAL GAINS

There are two particular points worth noting with respect to tax savings on income in the form of capital gains. First, the Capital Gains Exemption. The government has seen fit to encourage investment in certain capital properties by granting a Capital Gains Exemption to each and every individual Canadian. In basic terms, this exemption means that every man, woman and child may earn up to $100,000 in capital gains tax free. (These earnings are subject to certain adjustments, particularly those under the cumulative net investment loss rules, which need not be explored for present purposes. Note also that capital gains treatment may be denied by Revenue Canada if it determines you are in the *business* of buying and selling capital properties. Being in the *business* of buying and selling land is different from buying the odd piece and selling it at a profit, a capital gain. Professional advice is recommended here.)

Originally, the Capital Gains Exemption was set at $500,000. When it was reduced to $100,000, the $500,000 limit was retained for capital gains realized on the sale of the shares of qualified farm corporations and qualified small business corporations. As this is not a book on tax but rather wealth accumulation, these exceptions will not be explored here, other than to point out that using a corporate form for a main or side business may enable its owners to access the additional $400,000 Capital Gains Exemption if the shares of the corporation can be sold at a profit at some point down the road. Again, proper tax planning is recommended for those who may be in a position to take advantage of this rule.

It is sufficient for our purposes to point out that we have an additional incentive by way of the Capital Gains Exemption to purchase qualifying capital properties, thereby making such investments more attractive. It is also common wisdom that there is political pressure to remove the Capital Gains Exemption entirely and that therefore one should use this exemption sooner rather than later.

In other words, if it otherwise makes sense in your wealth accumulation program, you should realize your capital gains at the earliest possible opportunity and otherwise make investments where you anticipate making capital gains as early as possible in the wealth accumulation process. Those who hesitate may be lost.

Once you have exhausted your capital gains exemption, note that at present only three-quarters of capital gains are taxed. In other words, the income tax on capital gains is lower than tax on other forms of income such as interest income, rents and royalties.

The rationale behind this is that those who acquire capital properties such as stocks and real estate are presumably taking a greater risk than those who buy interest bearing instruments. This risk, so the thinking goes, should be rewarded. Hence the tax break.

In fact, one economic recovery strategy that gets trotted out by government and the opposition from time to time is to reduce the amount of capital gains subject to income tax to encourage these types of capital investments because they are seen as good for the economy.

At the same time, however, there are those who argue that it is generally the wealthier among us who invest in capital properties and in any event purchasing such properties is usually used as a tax planning device that leaves lower-income taxpayers carrying the bulk of the tax burden. Therefore, the argument goes, capital gains should be fully taxed. It is not necessary to resolve this argument here and it is sufficient to point out that income in the form of capital gains is still given favourable tax treatment. And again, this type of investment will reduce taxes and free up cash for further investment and wealth accumulation.

5

TAKING SHELTER

NOW THAT YOU HAVE CASH AVAILABLE FOR INVESTMENT, it's important to move it into a sheltered environment, using certain tax advantaged vehicles established under Canadian law to build wealth for retirement. These are essentially pension planning tools that have been made available to Canadians during the last 20 years. The government created them and generously gave up its claim to taxes on income derived from the money invested in them for the time being, in the hope that we would use them. Why was the government so generous?

By the 1970s it had become apparent that Canadians were not being particularly well served by the laws governing pension plans. Regulated at both the federal and provincial level, a patchwork of pension laws existed across the country. Most of the basic provisions of pension plans were left to negotiations between management and labour.

There were pension plans without indexation for inflation. There were plans that were anything but generous to a surviving spouse. And plans took years to "vest" (to lock in your benefit so that contributions to the pension plan from both you and your employer would benefit you).

Related to the issue of vesting was the general lack of portability of pension plans in this country. The plans were first created when Canadians stayed with a company throughout their working lives. We are now in an era of decreasing job security and the issue of portability has come to the fore.

Registered Retirement Savings Plans

Registered Retirement Savings Plans (RRSPs), which have been evolving since the late 1950s, were developed in recognition of the fact that Canadians without good company pension plans were in a disadvantaged position when it came to preparing adequately for their retirement. For many years the tax deductible contribution limit for RRSPs was 20% of earned income to a maximum of $3,500, not a particularly generous contribution limit, particularly when compared with the best company pension plans where both employer and employee were contributing.

As the years passed, the government began to realize that the aging population would pose a severe challenge to the social safety net, particularly the Old Age Pension and the Canada Pension Plan. It was also apparent that the Old Age Pension and Canada Pension Plan payments would be insufficient to maintain the reasonable living standards of Canadians as they entered their retirement years, particularly in light of the ever-increasing longevity of Canadian seniors.

Two classes of Canadians were emerging, those with good or reasonably good pension plans and those without. For those in the second group, it was painfully obvious that the low RRSP contribution limits would never permit tax sheltered savings to compound to a sufficient extent to place self-employed Canadians or those working for companies without adequate pension plans on anything close to an equal footing with those with good pension plans.

Recognizing these realities, the Government of Canada began the lengthy process of pension law reform. Along the way, RRSP limits were increased from $3,500 to an eventual limit of $15,500 per year, while the rule that limited deductible RRSP contributions to 20% of earned income was amended, reducing eligible contributions to 18% of earned income. It would now be necessary to have an earned income of $86,111.11 to be entitled to place the maximum $15,500 away in an RRSP ($86,111.11 x 18% = $15,500). Note that these dollar amounts will be indexed for inflation when the $15,500 contribution limit is reached.

This was a major step forward in pension law in Canada and, although the government has delayed the phasing in of the limits several times in an effort, ostensibly, to deal with the deficit, there is no doubt that many Canadians in all walks of life will, as a result of these reforms, be better able to look after themselves as they live longer and healthier lives.

Contributions made to an RRSP within the allowable limits generate a tax deduction. If you are in the 50% tax bracket, the tax saving will be approximately 50 cents on the dollar. In other words, to encourage contributions to an RRSP, the government in effect is willing to pay you (through tax savings) an amount equal to half of the RRSP contributions. This is extremely generous and makes the RRSP quite attractive on that basis alone.

Although it is no longer possible to deduct interest paid on monies borrowed to make annual RRSP contributions, it is common wisdom in the financial planning sector to advise clients who are unable to make their contributions to borrow and pay interest provided that the loan can be repaid within 12 months.

As noted in Chapter 4, from a wealth accumulation perspective, the RRSP is not merely a tax savings device, but also a tax deferral device, one that enables money to be placed in a tax sheltered environment so that it can grow in a compound way without the annual ravages of taxation. The earlier funds are placed in this environment the better, so that tax sheltered growth can begin. This is where the real power of the RRSP lies. Contributions to it enjoy compound growth free of the greatest wealth destroyer, taxation. In this tax sheltered environment, significant wealth can be accumulated.

It is disturbing to note that many eligible Canadians do not contribute to an RRSP. It is equally disturbing to note that many Canadians with RRSPs do not invest the money placed in them to achieve returns sufficient to overcome the long-term effects of that other wealth destroyer, inflation. All too often money is simply plunked into an RRSP for the immediate tax savings and then summarily ignored. If you behave in this fashion, you squander an enormous opportunity and should take steps immediately to rectify this situation.

The RRSP can and should be an important building block in the wealth accumulation process. The maximum contributions should be made regularly and the tax sheltered funds invested wisely to build a tax sheltered pool for retirement purposes.

Individual Pension Plans

For those with higher earned incomes, it may be beneficial to establish an executive pension plan, a vehicle with even greater potential than the RRSP. This type of pension planning arrangement has been commonly referred to as the Individual Pension Plan (IPP).

Note that one basic prerequisite for establishing an IPP is a master/servant relationship or, in common parlance, an employer/employee relationship. In simple terms, the IPP is only available to "employees," those generally in a T4 relationship with an "employer." And it is the employer, not the employee, who establishes the IPP. Hence the portability of the IPP, which may be transferred from one employer to another if the new employer is willing to offer one. If the new employer is not willing to do so, the individual has the choice of deferring the IPP pension or transferring the IPP pool to a locked-in RRSP within the limits provided by law. Any balance that may not be so transferred would be taxable, although other options may be available and should be discussed with a qualified adviser. Note that employers are increasingly willing to offer IPPs as an inducement to keeping highly skilled employees in their employ. It's a valuable employment benefit to have your own, individualized pension tailored to your personal needs.

For those with an incorporated business and for many in executive positions, having the corporation decide whether to offer an IPP does not pose a difficulty. The same is true of incorporated professionals, those whose professional associations or licensing bodies do not prohibit incorporation.

For those professionals such as dentists, physicians and lawyers (in those provinces where incorporation of their professional activities is not permitted), it may be possible to incorporate the non-professional, management aspects of the practice. In other words, "practice management" would, where appropriate, be incorporated and the professional's management services delivered through the management corporation. The purpose of such a management corporation would be twofold: first, to provide for the efficient management of the professional practice and, second, to provide a vehicle through which an IPP may be put in place to enable the professional to look after his or her long-term financial security.

It is worth noting that such professionals may have to pay GST on any monies paid as management and similar fees from their professional practice to their management corporation. To the extent that there are insufficient amounts of GST collected from those to whom services are provided to set off against this GST paid (as is the case with dentists and physicians in particular), this tax will reduce somewhat the attractiveness of the IPP. Nevertheless, the increased tax deductions and increased tax sheltered compounding still make the IPP an attractive and superior pension for professionals in these circumstances. There are also planning techniques that can offset and in some cases eliminate the impact of GST over time, a discussion of which exceeds our scope here. For all other employees, including incorporated professionals, owner-operators and executives, there is generally no GST issue with which to grapple and the benefit of the IPP in that regard is absolute.

Once an employer/employee relationship is identified (or established), the employer and employee must meet and work out the arrangements for the IPP. In the context of the owner-operator, incorporated professional or professional who has incorporated the management portion of the practice, this meeting must still take place.

The reason for the meeting is fundamental. It is the employer that establishes the IPP, not the individual. It is the employer, moreover, that should pay the cost of establishing, registering and maintaining the IPP. In this way, the cost of the IPP will be tax deductible because it is a business expense incurred on account of the employee. If it were determined the employee paid personally for the cost of the employer establishing and registering the IPP, it would not be tax deductible to the employer.

Furthermore, it is the employer that contributes to the IPP on the employee's behalf, with the employee's compensation package being negotiated accordingly. In this manner the appropriate salary, costs and contributions can be determined and the pension plan established.

If a self-directed IPP is selected, the employer would place the IPP contributions in a special IPP trust account with a financial institution for the purpose of receiving contributions to the IPP. In fact, in its legal essence, an IPP is a trust arrangement established by a trust agreement. In other words, it is a trust fund in favour of the employee and it is the employer that contributes to this trust fund on the employee's behalf as part of the employee's overall compensation package.

Should the employee die before receiving all of his or her pension benefits and therefore before exhausting the trust fund, the pension and benefit of the trust fund would typically go to the surviving spouse, and on that surviving spouse's death, to the employee's estate. (Note that the IPP rules relating to survivors—including spouses or other designated heirs—guarantee periods, survivor pensions, entitlements to surpluses and the like are more complex than summarized here. These rules should be explored with a qualified adviser.)

A question I am frequently asked at tax planning seminars and speaking engagements is whether establishing an IPP will preclude contributions to an RRSP. Is it possible to contribute to both? The answer is yes, to a limited extent. If you establish an IPP and contribute the maximum possible to it based on the highest allowable salary, you may not only keep your existing RRSP, you are permitted to contribute up to an additional $1,000 per year to it. In other words, when you establish an IPP, your RRSP is not collapsed or rolled over but will continue to exist. In this way, an attractive and fully tax sheltered IPP and RRSP fund may be built up over the years to maximize the tax sheltering advantages for future financial security.

In that regard, it may be advisable to treat this smaller RRSP tax sheltered growth fund somewhat differently from the main IPP pension fund. It may be advisable, for example, to be more aggressive or more adventurous with the RRSP fund than the IPP fund. Certainly having two funds (albeit one larger than the other), provides additional opportunity and incentive to diversify your portfolio.

Within specified limits, contributions are made to the IPP by your employer on your behalf. This provides an immediate tax saving. Funds then grow inside the IPP on a tax sheltered basis. Funds are, of course, taxable when removed from the IPP, as is the case with the RRSP.

Note that, while the IPP is beneficial for all income levels, the more you earn (up to approximately $87,000 a year) the greater the benefit will be. Note also, however, that there are set-up and maintenance costs (discussed below) that render the IPP less attractive and even unattractive for those with significantly lower annual incomes. It is not possible to identify a minimum annual income below which the IPP ceases to be attractive as set-up costs vary from case to case. Past service contributions (discussed below) and anticipated increases in annual compensation are also factors that may make the IPP attractive for those with annual incomes that otherwise appear short of the mark.

An IPP could be of value to executives, highly paid employees and the owner-operators of corporations. For others, the common wisdom is that a group RRSP or individual RRSPs would be a simpler solution. Even though a group pension plan may be beneficial depending on the circumstances, an IPP for specific individuals should not be ruled out.

The IPP is also a powerful tool for incorporated professionals. For those who are professionals who are not eligible to incorporate their particular profession you can still take advantage of the benefits of an IPP if the management aspects of your practice are incorporated. And for executives, highly paid employees, owner-operators, incorporated professionals and those professionals who incorporate the management aspects of their practices, the IPP is a tax deferral vehicle that, where it is appropriate, may be much superior to an RRSP.

First, the IPP is a "defined benefit" pension plan. A defined benefit pension plan is a pension plan with a precalculated, determined amount of pension (the defined benefit) payable at a specific retirement age. In other words, it is determined at the outset when a pension will be payable and how much that pension will be. It is not a "savings plan" like the RRSP where you don't have a specified benefit. By comparison, therefore, the IPP is truly an "individual" pension plan, one that can be tailored to the needs of the individual and, within the limits prescribed by law, may be amended from time to time or suspended as circumstances require.

The IPP is a "registered" pension plan (RPP). Generally, pension laws require that an RPP be registered federally and provincially. On filing an application for registration, the appropriate government departments will review the pension plan documents to ensure that they conform to applicable laws and regulations.

The IPP is creditor proof. Generally, an RRSP may be seized by creditors in satisfaction of a judgement against the RRSP's owner, although this may not be the case with respect to certain RRSPs on a group basis or available through the life insurance industry. The IPP, on the other hand, is free from the risk of seizure by creditors. In the event your business fails or you are hit with a sizeable lawsuit for whatever reason, the money in your IPP is not subject to seizure because it is truly a pension plan (RPP), although money in an IPP is an asset subject to division under matrimonial law in the same fashion as any other pension plan.

An IPP is highly regulated and this is often seen as a disadvantage. Because it is a pension plan, it is governed by pension regulations at both the federal and provincial levels. The RRSP is simpler to establish and maintain. In addition to the registration of a written pension plan noted at the outset, annual forms must be filed to maintain the IPP's registered status.

The law requires that, at the outset and periodically thereafter, a person called an actuary (a professional qualified to practice in this statistical field) must analyse the IPP to ensure that the pension target (the defined benefit) to be paid on retirement will be achieved. It is not simply a matter of dumping money in and watching it grow in a tax sheltered environment. Yes, money is contributed every year and, yes, it does grow in a tax sheltered environment, but because there must be a pension of a defined size at the other end, there must be enough money in the IPP fund to accomplish this defined benefit objective.

As I noted, the highly regulated nature of IPPs is often viewed as a disadvantage, but it can be seen the other way. It is helpful for most of us to have the periodic services of an actuary to ensure that the IPP is on target, to ensure that the rate of return achieved to date is sufficient to deliver the pension benefit promised. One of the major drawbacks with savings plans such as RRSPs is that they underperform, generally because they are ignored, and the owners of RRSPs have literally no idea how much pension benefit will be available at retirement. The IPP, on the contrary, imposes a certain discipline, the discipline of an actuary's periodic valuation, and this is particularly attractive for those who would be inclined to pay too little attention to such a retirement vehicle. Are you a member of this group?

Additionally, the funds placed inside an IPP are "locked in." It's not possible, as it is with an RRSP, to withdraw funds from an IPP from time to time except for retirement purposes. It is a pension plan and the funds are for your retirement. Again, this feature is sometimes viewed as a disadvantage. Although it does reduce your liquidity, this feature generally is an advantage because, for many of us, the harder it is to get at our money, the better off we will be. Withdrawing funds from an RRSP, even small amounts, greatly reduces the compound tax sheltered potential. Funds that have been carefully set aside in an RRSP can be nibbled at until they are depleted. Once funds are successfully placed out of the reach of annual taxation, it would be a shame to bring them back out again earlier and lose the carefully planned, tax-sheltered advantages.

That said, it is clear that there may be situations in your life, including the purchase of a first home, that would make liquidity a desirable thing, and in those cases the ability to withdraw investment funds is important. To that extent, if you choose an IPP, make sure that some of your investments are accessible and not locked inside an IPP.

The most obvious difference between the IPP and the RRSP for the typical executive, professional or business person is immediate tax savings. Depending on your age, it is possible to contribute more tax deductible dollars to an IPP than to an RRSP. The contribution limit increases with your age. Each year, a larger amount can be contributed. This is not true of RRSPs.

It is common wisdom, moreover, that you should be at least in your late 30s before establishing an IPP, but there is no hard and fast rule. Prior to that age, the amount that you would need to contribute to an IPP to meet pension targets (the defined benefit) could actually be less than your allowable RRSP contributions. In other words, in the early years, contribute to an RRSP to obtain the maximum tax savings. At a certain point in your late 30s or beyond, the establishment of an IPP could be much more attractive.

As with RRSPs, it is possible to have a self-directed IPP and generally to make the same types of investments in the same manner as you would with an RRSP. The tax sheltered nature of the IPP and the RRSP is therefore basically the same, except that the potential exists with the IPP to have substantially more money earning income that is sheltered from taxation.

Now to the issue of "past service contributions," which may dramatically increase the attractiveness of IPPs in appropriate circumstances. Past service contributions relate to the contributions that may be made to your IPP based on your past service, that is, employment income earned in years prior to the year the IPP is established. There are certain legal limitations on past service contributions and they must be calculated by an actuary. Ask your IPP adviser about the possibility of past service contributions when investigating whether or not an IPP is for you.

An IPP Analysis   To assist you in developing some appreciation of the IPP and its advantages and possible disadvantages, a series of tables has been prepared. The tables are of two basic types: projections of the assets you may build up using an IPP and projections of the benefit you may receive from your IPP on retirement.

To assist you further in your comparison, each of the IPP asset projection tables and IPP benefit projection tables includes an equivalent RRSP asset projection and RRSP benefit projection. In this way, you can compare the IPP with the RRSP and be in a position to make a more informed choice.

Tables were prepared for individuals ranging in age from 30 to 65 years. The age of 40 was then arbitrarily selected as the age for discussion purposes. You will see, therefore, a series of tables calculated at age 40 to highlight the differences that occur when various factors concerning IPPs are taken into account.

Let us begin with a Canadian male who is 40 years of age, assuming he has the earned income needed to support an IPP (an income of $90,000 plus). The IPP asset projection is shown in the table opposite.

Note that in this table there are several columns as follows:

> YEAR: These columns begin in 1994, the year of the publication of this book, and proceed approximately in five year increments until the year our contributor turns 71, when contributions to an IPP are no longer permitted.
>
> AGE: The individual's age, in this case commencing at 40, through to the age of 71.
>
> IPP CONTRIBUTIONS: The tax deductible amount that may be contributed to an IPP annually. At age 40, for example, $15,182 may be contributed (for an immediate tax saving of $7,591 for an individual in the 50% marginal tax bracket).
>
> IPP FUND AT END OF YEAR: The size of the IPP asset fund at the end of the year. At the end of the first year in the above example the amount in the fund is $15,741. How was this figure calculated? First, the interest rate assumed in all of these examples (unless otherwise stated) is 7.5% per annum. Why this particular rate of interest? Because this is the percentage of growth anticipated at present by pension legislation (or, more precisely, a rate of return 3.5% over the established inflation rate

IPP ASSET PROJECTION
FOR A PLAN BEGUN AT AGE 40

		IPP	
Year	**Age**	**Contributions**	**Fund at year-end**
1994	40	15,182	15,741
2000	46	24,430	177,559
2005	51	34,637	435,307
2010	56	49,290	881,302
2015	61	70,326	1,630,639
2020	66	96,547	2,858,847
2025	71[1]	111,295	4,502,525

		RRSP and GIC			
Year	**Age**	**Contributions RRSP**	**Contributions GIC**	**RRSP Fund at year-end**	**GIC Fund at year-end**
1994	40	13,500	841	13,997	856
2000	46	19,202	2,614	146,575	13,882
2005	51	25,096	4,770	345,555	37,495
2010	56	32,799	8,245	672,695	81,702
2015	61	42,868	13,729	1,196,558	160,002
2020	66	56,026	20,261	2,019,483	291,408
2025	71[1]	73,224	19,036	3,293,498	458,685

(1) IPP advantage over an RRSP at age 71 without considering the GIC Fund: $1,209,027 (36.71%). IPP advantage over an RRSP at age 71 if RRSP contributor has an additional GIC fund: $750,342 (20.00%)

which, at the time of writing, is 4%). But 7.5% growth in one year on an IPP contribution of $15,182 does not equal $15,741, you say. No, it doesn't, because the computer program that generates these projections assumes that you will make your IPP contribution halfway through the year, to average the fact that some individuals contribute at the beginning, some at the end, others monthly and so on. Even then, you will notice a few dollars in the difference. The computer calculates more precisely than a pocket calculator.

RRSP CONTRIBUTIONS: The tax deductible amount that you may contribute annually to an RRSP. In 1994 the contribution limit is $13,500 for Canadians of all ages. In 1995 it is anticipated it will be $14,500 and in 1996 $15,500. After that, the law prescribes that it be indexed to wage inflation which is assumed to be 5.5% per year. Therefore, in the year 2000, for example, you will be entitled to contribute $19,202 to an RRSP.

GIC CONTRIBUTIONS: This one takes some explanation. What is a Guaranteed Investment Certificate (GIC) doing in the middle of our IPP/RRSP comparison? Well, in order to be fair to RRSPs and to enable you to compare apples with apples as the saying goes, we needed a mechanism to take into account the difference between the IPP contributions and the RRSP contributions. That money difference doesn't just disappear, presumably. If you choose the RRSP over the IPP you'll have that extra amount that could have been put into the IPP left over, right? So we've taken it into account by assuming you'd buy a GIC with it and let that GIC grow for you. To account for the fact, however, that a GIC is not a tax sheltered instrument and that you won't save 50 cents of every dollar you put into it in taxes, we divided the amount of the GIC contributions column in half ($15,182 - $13,500 = $1,682 ÷ 2 = $841, the amount in the Contributions GIC column).

RRSP FUND AT YEAR-END: The size of the RRSP asset fund at the end of the year, assuming again the contributions are made mid-year and the annual rate of return is 7.5%. For example, at the end of the first year, $13,997 is the RRSP asset balance.

GIC FUND AT YEAR-END: Let's not forget our unsheltered monies out there struggling in a fully taxable environment. By the end of the first year they have been growing for six months and half of that growth has been paid in taxes. In the first year of the example, therefore, the $841 has grown to $856.

The IPP asset projection starting at age 40, then, takes us in intervals of five years through to the age of 71. Now, I understand that you plan to retire at 55 (or whatever). In fact, the trend in recent years is to retire early. There are those who argue, however, that of necessity—what with increasing longevity and the need to accumulate more wealth and the anticipated shortage of skilled people as the baby boomers pass through into retirement—this trend will actually be reversed and we will begin to work longer. In any event, the law permits IPP and RRSP contributions to age 71, so we have calculated the amounts to age 71.

You will also note that at the bottom of the table footnotes show the dollar figure and the percentage by which the IPP is superior, *without* the GIC fund taken into account and *with* the GIC fund. Why this distinction?

The answer lies in the realm of human nature. If you contributed $13,500 to an RRSP instead of $15,182 to an IPP, would you *really* invest the difference in a GIC, or anywhere else for that matter, or would you let it slip through your fingers? Hopefully, reading this book will change your answer, but from my experience most of you will let it slip away.

If you think you would fail to invest the difference and if you started at age 40 as in the table, you would be $1,209,027 or 36.71% ahead with the IPP at the age of 71 ($4,502,525 IPP fund - $3,293,498 RRSP fund = $1,209,027 ahead). If you invested the difference in a vehicle such as a GIC at the same rate of return, this IPP advantage would be reduced to $750,342 or 20.00%.

Now to the IPP benefit projection, again assuming the plan was started at age 40. Study the table below.

Note that this is the table that indicates how much pension our 40 year old can expect to receive at various ages. There are five columns from left to right as follows:

> YEAR: The earliest age at which you can take your IPP pension (at least in the most restrictive provinces) is 55. Therefore, we start at age 55 in all our examples. In the case of a 40 year old, age 55 comes in the year 2009 (1994 plus 15).

IPP BENEFIT PROJECTION
FOR A PLAN BEGUN AT AGE 40

| Year | Age | IPP | RRSP and GIC | |
		Annual Pension	Annual "Pension" RRSP	Annual "Pension" GIC
2009	55	68,242	52,500	6,243
2015	61	159,052	116,712	15,607
2020	66	311,893	220,320	31,792
2025	71	563,070	411,874	57,362

AGE: The examples are prepared approximately in five year intervals to the age of 71, at which time the pension benefit must be taken.

IPP ANNUAL PENSION: If our 40 year old retires at 55 after contributing for only 15 years, he will receive a pension from the IPP of $68,242 a year. If he works to age 61, however, the pension jumps to $159,052 a year. Look at the pension at ages 66 or 71, all calculated based on the life expectancy for a Canadian male. (Later we will also look at an example for a Canadian female.)

RRSP ANNUAL "PENSION": Since the RRSP is a savings plan and not a defined benefit pension plan, there is no "pension" as such. But to facilitate comparison, we have calculated the equivalent of a pension for the RRSP on the same assumptions that were employed for the IPP. Note that the RRSP pension at age 55 is $52,500, $15,742 lower than the IPP pension of $68,242 per year. Compare the results at ages 61, 66 and 71.

GIC ANNUAL "PENSION": Let's not forget the GIC fund building in a fully taxable environment for those of us with RRSPs and the discipline to invest those additional dollars. If our 40 year old retires at age 55, the GIC fund will produce an income (or a "pension") of $6,243 per year.

Now, three additional points need to be made about these two IPP tables before proceeding further, to round out the picture so that we can build on these examples. First, they have been calculated on the assumption that our 40 year old has an earned income of $90,000-plus a year in 1994, indexed yearly thereafter at the rate of 5.5% (assumed wage inflation) per year. Although this salary level is a bit above the usual maximum of $86,111 needed to make the maximum contributions at the outset, our actuaries indicate that starting at $90,000 ensures adequate funding throughout. As indicated earlier in the chapter, the IPP is superior to the RRSP at all income levels but (subject to absorbing set-up and maintenance costs, discussed below) this superiority is greatest at the highest eligible income level.

Second, when you contribute the maximum to an IPP you are also still permitted to contribute an additional $1,000 per year to an RRSP. All of the IPP asset projections in this book include this additional $1,000 in the IPP contributions column, and in the IPP benefit projections the "pension" resulting from the fund generated from these additional annual $1,000 contributions is included in the IPP annual pension column.

Third, we will provide below examples of what happens to your IPP contributions if you earn more or less than the anticipated 7.5% rate of return on your IPP investments annually. As you will see, if you earn less than 7.5%, a funding deficiency will result—your IPP Fund will be lower than it should be. If you earn more than 7.5%, a funding surplus will result. Even at 7.5%, however, a modest surplus will occur in the later years, at or near age 71, but this anomaly has been ignored in our comparisons. Deficiencies and surpluses, therefore, will be discussed only in those examples provided below specifically for that purpose.

Before we look at the IPP potential for individuals starting an IPP anywhere between the ages of 30 and 65 (yes, it is possible to start that late), there are four different points of comparison that should be made at the age of 40, the age we have selected for making the bulk of our comparisons, as follows.

1. What if the participant is female?

2. How do set-up and maintenance costs affect the performance of the plan?

3. What if there is a performance deficiency? (two examples)

4. What if there is a performance surplus? (two examples)

First, take a look at our IPP asset projection and our IPP
benefit projection for a female participant on pages 110 and
111.

You will note that the IPP asset projection table for a
female participant is identical to the IPP asset projection table
for our 40 year old male participant. As you would expect,
they both accumulate the same amounts in their IPP and
RRSP funds. But then compare the IPP benefit projections,
for example at age 71. The female participant will receive an
IPP annual pension of $481,429 whereas the male participant
will receive $563,070. Why the difference? Because according
to the actuarial mortality assumptions, a female will live six to
seven years longer than a male.

Next, we look at the impact of set-up and maintenance
costs. Study the two tables on pages 112 and 113, particularly
the new column entitled "costs," that is, the cost of setting up
and maintaining your IPP.

As discussed earlier, there is a cost to setting up and maintaining an IPP. Although these costs will vary from place to
place and time to time, we have assumed here that the cost of
setting up the IPP will be $3,500, a one-time cost incurred at
the outset. We have assumed annual maintenance costs to be
$1,000 and the cost of the tri-annual actuarial valuation (the
cost of having an actuary review the IPP every third year to
determine if you are on course for achieving your defined

IPP ASSET PROJECTION
FEMALE PARTICIPANT

FOR A PLAN BEGUN AT AGE 40

		IPP	
Year	Age	Contributions	Fund at year-end
1994	40	15,182	15,741
2000	46	24,430	177,559
2005	51	34,637	435,307
2010	56	49,290	881,302
2015	61	70,326	1,630,639
2020	66	96,547	2,858,847
2025	71[1]	111,295	4,502,525

		RRSP and GIC		
Year	Age	Contributions RRSP	Contributions GIC	RRSP Fund at year-end	GIC Fund at year-end
1994	40	13,500	841	13,997	856
2000	46	19,202	2,614	146,575	13,882
2005	51	25,096	4,770	345,555	37,495
2010	56	32,799	8,245	672,695	81,702
2015	61	42,868	13,729	1,196,558	160,002
2020	66	56,026	20,261	2,019,483	291,408
2025	71[1]	73,224	19,036	3,293,498	458,685

(1) IPP advantage over an RRSP at age 71 without considering the GIC Fund: $1,209,027 (36.71%). IPP advantage over an RRSP at age 71 if RRSP contributor has an additional GIC fund: $750,342 (20.00%).

benefit) to be $1,000 every third year. Over a typical three year period through the life of the IPP, therefore, you will spend $4,000 in annual maintenance costs ($1,000 x 3 + $1,000 for actuarial valuation). On average these costs will be $1,333 per year and this amount has been assumed throughout, indexed for inflation at 4% per year. That is why, in the year 2000, these ongoing costs are $1,687 ($1,333 x 4% compounded annually x 6 years). You will find this amount for the year 2000 in the column entitled "costs," and will see that it is indexed for inflation thereafter. For the first year, 1994, you will see in that same column the $3,500 set-up cost.

Why have we placed the set-up and maintenance costs in the column on the RRSP side of the table? Isn't the cost of an IPP something that should show up on the IPP side? The logic of placing IPP costs on the RRSP side is to assist in comparing the IPP with the RRSP. Recall that we are using the concept of a GIC to enable us to demonstrate certain differences between these two tax sheltered vehicles. For exam-

IPP BENEFIT PROJECTION, FEMALE PARTICIPANT
FOR A PLAN BEGUN AT AGE 40

		IPP	RRSP and GIC	
Year	Age	Annual Pension	Annual "Pension" RRSP	Annual "Pension" GIC
2009	55	63,042	48,499	5,768
2015	61	143, 093	105,001	14,041
2020	66	272,848	192,739	27,812
2025	71	481,429	352,155	49,045

IPP ASSET PROJECTION

FOR A PLAN BEGUN AT AGE 40

(with set-up and maintenance costs)

		IPP	
Year	**Age**	**Contributions**	**Fund at year-end**
1994	40	15,182	15,741
2000	46	24,430	177,559
2005	51	34,637	435,307
2010	56	49,290	881,302
2015	61	70,326	1,630,639
2020	66	96,547	2,858,847
2025	71[1]	111,295	4,502,525

		RRSP and GIC				
Year	**Age**	**Contributions RRSP**	**Contributions GIC**	**Costs**	**RRSP Fund at year end**	**GIC Fund at year end**
1994	40	13,500	2,591	3,500	13,997	2,639
2000	45	19,202	3,458	1,687	146,575	21,229
2005	51	25,096	5,797	2,053	345,555	51,529
2010	56	32,799	9,494	2,497	672,695	104,902
2015	61	42,868	15,248	3,038	1,196,558	195,590
2020	66	56,026	22,109	3,697	2,019,483	343,556
2025	71[1]	73,224	21,284	4,497	3,293,498	532,769

(1) IPP advantage over an RRSP at age 71 without considering the GIC Fund: $1,209,027 (36.71%). IPP advantage over an RRSP at age 71 if RRSP contributor has an additional GIC fund: $676,258 (17.67%)

ple, in the table on page 103 we added to the GIC fund the
after tax difference between the IPP and RRSP contribution
limits. After all, if you choose the RRSP over the IPP you will
have contributed less than you could have if you had chosen
the IPP. The excess has to go somewhere and we created the
GIC columns for this purpose.

It's the same with costs. We divide them in half (they're tax
deductible) and place them in the GIC column and let them
grow in a fully taxable environment. This is what you would
do (at least in theory) if you chose an RRSP over an IPP and
were a disciplined person. You'd invest (in a taxable environment like a GIC) not only the extra money you would have
been able to contribute to an IPP had you established one,
but also the set-up and maintenance costs you would have
had to spend on the IPP. Therefore, to get the $2,591 amount
in the Contributions GIC column for the year 1994, for
example, add half the $3,500 in the costs column to the $841

IPP BENEFIT PROJECTION

FOR A PLAN BEGUN AT AGE 40

(with set-up and maintenance costs)

| | | IPP | RRSP and GIC | |
Year	Age	Annual Pension	Annual "Pension" RRSP	Annual "Pension" GIC
2009	55	68,242	52,500	8,111
2015	61	159,052	116,712	19,078
2020	66	311,893	220,320	37,481
2025	71	563,070	411,874	66,626

we already had in the GIC Contributions column in the table on page 103.

Note that the GIC fund in the final column now grows to $532,769 by the end of the participant's 71st year. In our original example (on page 103) the amount was $458,685, as no costs were included there. Then look at the bottom of the present IPP asset projection example (page 112), where the overall IPP advantage is calculated for you. Note that at age 71, *without* the additional GIC fund taken into account, the IPP advantage remains at $1,209,027 or 36.71% as it had in the original example. But when the GIC fund *is* taken into account, the investment income generated by funds that would be spent otherwise on IPP costs reduces the IPP advantage from the $750,342 or 20% as in the original example to $676,258 or 17.67%, 2.33% less for an individual who begins an IPP at 40 years of age.

Now compare the IPP benefit projection with costs taken into account (page 113), with the original IPP benefit projection without costs on page 106. You will note that the effect of this 2.33% difference shows up in the fifth column, the GIC annual "pension" column. The GIC annual pension at age 71, for example, will now be $66,626 instead of $57,362.

Next, two examples to highlight the issue known as deficiency or deficit. Remember that the primary objective of an IPP, other than your objective of saving extra tax along the way as a direct result of the larger annual contributions, is to reach your defined benefit or pension target. You must achieve 7.5% growth in the IPP per year to accomplish this. What if you fall short? The easy answer is to find a new financial planner. There is no way you should be falling below 7.5%. If you are, something is wrong with your investment strategy. But if you do fall short, it will eventually be highlighted by your actuary on one or more of the tri-annual valuations and, unless you make arrangements to amend the plan, the shortfall must be made up by contributing extra tax deductible dollars. This could be done in one year or over a number of years.

For those of you who have good cash flows who are looking for places to shelter additional tax deductible dollars, this is not such a bad thing, although you should be concerned that your IPP investments are underachieving so badly. For others, if the shortfall is temporary it may be advisable to borrow from time to time to ensure the maximum possible contributions, particularly if the loan will be repaid within 12 months. Actually, it is the corporation that would borrow since it is the corporation that establishes the plan and contributes to it. Your compensation package with the corporation would be negotiated and adjusted accordingly, not a difficult thing to do in most situations, particularly if it is your own corporation. It generally makes financial sense to borrow in this fashion as, in the case of the IPP (unlike the RRSP), the interest on such borrowings should be tax deductible.

With that introduction, refer now to the two pairs of tables that follow. They have been calculated on the assumptions that you have underachieved by averaging 6.5% per year in the first set of tables and 5.5%, a dismal rate of return, in the second.

Note that there is now an additional column in the IPP asset projections because there are two IPP contribution columns, one without taking the deficit into account and one with it. Note also that the projection now includes additional years and is not limited to every fifth year. The reason for this

IPP ASSET PROJECTION
FOR A PLAN BEGUN AT AGE 40
(6.5% Annual Rate of Return)

IPP				
Year	Age	IPP Contrib. (no deficit)	IPP Contrib. (to cover deficit)	Fund at year-end
1994	40	15,182	15,182	15,667
1997	43	19,860	20,618	80,859
2000	46	24,430	27,274	175,775
2003	49	30,107	36,040	311,030
2005	51	34,637	34,637	424,012
2006	52	37,159	47,513	500,605
2009	55	45,921	62,488	762,889
2010	56	49,290	49,290	863,343
2012	58	56,805	81,990	1,121,991
2015	61	70,326	107,332	1,609,441
2018	64	87,124	140,200	2,266,362
2020	66	96,547	96,547	2,773,055
2024	70	108,379	1,000	3,928,369
2025	71[1]	111,295	31,427	4,216,145

RRSP and GIC				
Year	Age	Contributions RRSP	Contributions GIC	RRSP Fund at year-end	GIC Fund at year-end
1994	40	13,500	841	13,932	854
1997	43	16,353	2,133	67,712	6,232
2000	46	19,202	4,036	141,807	15,550
2003	49	22,548	6,746	241,765	30,699
2005	51	25,096	4,770	326,259	42,035
2006	52	26,476	10,518	374,789	54,089
2009	55	31,089	15,699	549,894	88,209
2010	56	32,799	8,245	619,485	100,209
2012	58	36,507	22,742	778,342	139,541
2015	61	42,868	32,232	1,074,176	211,557
2018	64	50,337	44,931	1,454,873	312,451
2020	66	56,026	20,261	1,766,338	374,911
2024	70	69,407	(34,203)	2,562,941	456,451
2025	71[1]	73,224	(20,898)	2,805,099	450,051

(1) IPP advantage over an RRSP at age 71 without considering the GIC Fund: $1,411,046 (50.30%). IPP advantage over an RRSP at age 71 if RRSP contributor has an additional GIC fund: $960,995 (29.52%)

is that the deficiencies occur in certain years and not others. To highlight when this occurs, each of these years is included and identified by a box.

In the first set of projections (at 6.5% return), for example, a deficit occurs eight times, at ages 43, 46, 49, 52, 55, 58, 61 and 64, in other words every third year. No attempt has been made in this example, for simplicity's sake, to spread out the impact of these deficiencies; they have been absorbed entirely in the year in which they arise.

Note the impact of these deficiencies on the GIC contribution and GIC fund columns. A disciplined RRSP contributor would have to invest that much more money in a taxable environment such as a GIC to equal the dollars at work in an IPP, in this case an IPP with a deficiency. The impact of this deficiency is actually quite modest at 6.5% (a GIC fund of $450,051 at the end of the 71st year as compared with $458,685 at the end of the 71st year in the example given at the outset). This is in large measure because of a surplus that

IPP BENEFIT PROJECTION
FOR A PLAN BEGUN AT AGE 40
(6.5% Annual Rate of Return)

| | | IPP | RRSP and GIC | |
Year	Age	Annual Pension	Annual "Pension" RRSP	Annual "Pension" GIC
2009	55	62,047	44,724	7,234
2015	61	145,998	97,442	19,191
2020	66	283,952	180,868	38,390
2025	71	499,478	332,314	53,317

IPP ASSET PROJECTION

FOR A PLAN BEGUN AT AGE 40

(5.5% Annual Rate of Return)

IPP				
Year	Age	IPP Contrib. (no deficit)	IPP Contrib. (to cover deficit)	Fund at year-end
1994	40	15,182	15,182	15,594
1997	43	19,860	21,370	80,156
2000	46	24,430	30,066	174,028
2003	49	30,107	41,839	307,686
2005	51	34,637	34,637	413,028
2006	52	37,159	57,612	494,920
2009	55	45,921	78,632	753,869
2010	56	49,290	49,290	845,958
2012	58	56,805	106,514	1,108,312
2015	61	70,326	143,350	1,589,357
2018	64	87,124	191,842	2,237,577
2020	66	96,547	96,547	2,691,054
2024	70	108,379	102,525	3,790,493
2025	71[1]	111,295	111,295	4,113,285

RRSP and GIC				
Year	Age	Contributions RRSP	Contributions GIC	RRSP Fund at year-end	GIC Fund at year-end
1994	40	13,500	841	13,866	852
1997	43	16,353	2,509	66,451	6,562
2000	46	19,202	5,432	137,198	17,170
2003	49	22,548	9,646	230,582	35,067
2005	51	25,096	4,770	308,197	46,285
2006	52	26,476	15,568	352,342	63,339
2009	55	31,089	23,771	509,534	106,129
2010	56	32,799	8,245	571,248	117,405
2012	58	36,507	35,004	710,807	168,967
2015	61	42,868	50,241	966,751	259,192
2018	64	50,337	70,753	1,290,307	386,496
2020	66	56,026	20,261	1,551,236	449,662
2024	70	69,407	16,559	2,206,869	582,323
2025	71[1]	73,224	19,036	2,403,457	617,633

(1) IPP advantage over an RRSP at age 71 without considering the GIC Fund: $1,709,828 (71.14%). IPP advantage over an RRSP at age 71 if RRSP contributor has an additional GIC Fund: $1,092,195 (36.15%)

shows up in the 70th and 71st years despite the fact that we have been running a deficit all that time. This makes no sense, you say? Recall that we discussed the anomaly of a surplus at 7.5%, too. In reality, your actuary will smooth most or all of this out on tri-annual valuations by working with you in light of the actual investment results you are achieving.

But in the pair of examples at 5.5%, the impact of the deficiency on the GIC fund column is more noticeable. Since the deficiencies at a 5.5% rate of return are greater than at 6.5%, the gap between the IPP and RRSP contributions widens. More dollars would theoretically go to the GIC fund to enable us to keep comparing apples with apples. Note therefore at age 71 a GIC fund of $617,633 at 5.5% instead of $450,051 at 6.5%.

To be consistent, not only your IPP investment earnings have been reduced to 6.5% and 5.5% in these tables. To keep comparing apples with apples, we have assumed that your RRSP and GIC funds are also only earning 6.5% and 5.5%.

IPP BENEFIT PROJECTION
FOR A PLAN BEGUN AT AGE 40
(5.5% Annual Rate of Return)

Year	Age	IPP Annual Pension	RRSP and GIC Annual "Pension" RRSP	RRSP and GIC Annual "Pension" GIC
2009	55	56,079	37,904	7,895
2015	61	133,433	81,162	21,760
2020	66	257,636	148,512	43,050
2025	71	460,252	268,933	69,109

IPP ASSET PROJECTION
FOR A PLAN BEGUN AT AGE 40
(8.5% Annual Rate of Return)

IPP				
Year	Age	IPP Contrib. (no surplus)	IPP Contrib. (when there is a surplus)	Fund at year-end
1994	40	15,182	15,182	15,814
2000	46	24,430	24,430	183,418
2005	51	34,637	34,637	460,445
2010	56	49,290	49,290	954,746
2015	61	70,326	64,935	1,804,010
2018	64	87,124	54,228	2,545,014
2020	66[1]	96,547	96,547	3,202,386
2021	67	99,516	1,000	3,475,630
2022	68	102,482	1,000	3,772,101
2023	69	105,439	15,009	4,108,363
2024	70	108,379	1,000	4,458,615
2025	71[2]	111,295	1,000	4,838,640

RRSP and GIC					
Year	Age	Contributions RRSP	Contributions GIC	RRSP Fund at year-end	GIC Fund at year-end
1994	40	13,500	841	14,062	859
2000	46	19,202	2,614	151,510	14,086
2005	51	25,096	4,770	366,171	38,387
2010	56	32,799	8,245	731,416	84,316
2015	61	42,868	11,034	1,336,123	163,568
2018	64	50,337	1,946	1,868,428	221,897
2020	66[1]	56,026	20,261	2,317,937	283,389
2021	67	59,108	(29,054)	2,576,530	265,768
2022	68	62,358	(30,679)	2,860,490	245,739
2023	69	65,788	(25,390)	3,172,159	230,259
2024	70	69,407	(34,203)	3,514,089	205,123
2025	71[2]	73,224	(36,112)	3,889,059	176,969

(1) IPP advantage over an RRSP at age 66 without considering the GIC Fund: $884,449 (38.16%). IPP advantage over an RRSP at age 66 if RRSP contributor has an additional GIC Fund: $601,060 (23.11%).
(2) IPP advantage over an RRSP at age 71 without considering the GIC Fund: $949,581 (24.42%). IPP advantage over an RRSP at age 71 if RRSP contributor has an additional GIC Fund: $772,612 (19.00%).

To make a comparison across the board of the long-term effect of achieving these lower rates of return, therefore, look at the bottom portion of both the 6.5% projection and the 5.5% projection to see the effect of deficiency on the IPP advantage at age 71 *without* and *with* the GIC fund taken into account. At 6.5%, the IPP advantage without the GIC fund is $1,411,046 or 50.3% and with the GIC fund is $960,995 or 29.52%. At 5.5%, the IPP advantage without GIC fund is $1,709,828 or 71.14% and with the GIC fund is $1,092,195 or 36.15%. Compare this with the IPP advantage in the example at the outset, which was $1,209,027 or 36.71% without the GIC fund and $750,342 or 20% with it. The IPP advantage increases as deficiencies increase.

Before leaving the issue of deficiencies, compare the IPP benefit projections at 6.5% and 5.5% with the projection at the outset (page 106). As you would expect, the IPP annual pension and RRSP annual "pension" stay the same. The dif-

IPP BENEFIT PROJECTION
FOR A PLAN BEGUN AT AGE 40
(8.5% Annual Rate of Return)

Year	Age	IPP	RRSP and GIC	
		Annual Pension	Annual "Pension" RRSP	Annual "Pension" GIC
2009	55	79,481	61,344	6,950
2015	61	188,357	139,505	17,078
2020	66	370,910	268,470	32,823
2025	71	636,999	511,988	23,298

IPP ASSET PROJECTION

FOR A PLAN BEGUN AT AGE 40 (9.5% Annual Rate of Return)

IPP

Year	Age	IPP Contrib. (no surplus)	IPP Contrib. (when there is a surplus)	Fund at year-end
1994	40	15,182	15,182	15,886
2000	46	24,430	24,430	189,477
2005	51	34,637	34,637	487,269
2009	55	45,921	37,038	889,391
2010	56	49,290	49,290	1,025,460
2012	58	56,805	1,000	1,291,227
2013	59	60,990	59,481	1,476,137
2015	61	70,326	1,000	1,846,010
2016	62	75,526	61,148	2,085,368
2018	64	87,124	1,000	2,594,399
2019	65	93,583	82,069	2,926,747
2020	66[1]	96,547	96,547	3,305,816
2021	67	99,516	1,000	3,620,915
2022	68	102,482	1,000	3,965,949
2023	69	105,439	1,000	4,343,760
2024	70	108,379	1,000	4,757,464
2025	71[2]	111,295	1,000	5,210,469

RRSP and GIC

Year	Age	Contributions RRSP	Contributions GIC	RRSP Fund at year-end	GIC Fund at year-end
1994	40	13,500	841	14,127	861
2000	46	19,202	2,614	156,616	14,293
2005	51	25,096	4,770	388,198	39,306
2009	55	31,089	2,974	695,817	70,494
2010	56	32,799	8,245	796,242	82,282
2012	58	36,507	(17,753)	1,032,565	81,928
2013	59	38,514	10,483	1,170,961	96,549
2015	61	42,868	(20,934)	1,495,427	97,838
2016	62	45,225	7,961	1,684,817	110,634
2018	64	50,337	(24,668)	2,127,482	114,051
2019	65	53,105	14,482	2,385,164	134,291
2020	66[1]	56,026	20,261	2,670,381	161,405
2021	67	59,108	(29,054)	2,985,919	139,336
2022	68	62,358	(30,679)	3,334,835	114,555
2023	69	65,788	(32,394)	3,720,486	86,842
2024	70	69,407	(34,203)	4,146,561	55,961
2025	71[2]	73,224	(36,112)	4,617,108	21,660

(1) IPP advantage over an RRSP at age 66 without considering the GIC Fund: $635,435 (23.80%). IPP advantage over an RRSP at age 66 if RRSP contributor has an additional GIC Fund: $474,030 (16.74%)
(2) IPP advantage over an RRSP at age 71 without considering the GIC Fund: $593,361 (12.85%). IPP advantage over an RRSP ata ge 71 if RRSP contributor has an additonal GIC Fund: $571,701 (12.32%)

ferences caused by the deficits show up in the GIC annual "pension."

Next, examples of surplus, where your IPP performs better than the 7.5% anticipated. These examples are calculated at 8.5% (pages 120 and 121) and 9.5% (opposite and below).

Now that you have become adept at reading IPP projections (something I suppose you never imagined you'd become adept at) you can see that the issue of surplus is somewhat the reverse of that of the issue of deficiency. You are overachieving instead of underachieving, earning annual rates above the anticipated 7.5%. You must scale back your annual contributions or you will exceed your defined benefit. This will certainly be a pleasure for those experiencing cash flow shortages but will reduce tax deductible contributions for those looking to plunk the most possible tax deductible dollars into this tax sheltered environment. Reductions in your contributions may be made in one year or smoothed out over a number of years in consultation with your actuary.

IPP BENEFIT PROJECTION
FOR A PLAN BEGUN AT AGE 40
(9.5% Annual Rate of Return)

Year	Age	IPP Annual Pension	RRSP and GIC Annual "Pension" RRSP	Annual "Pension" GIC
2009	55	91,239	71,381	7,232
2015	61	205,469	166,448	10,890
2020	66	405,155	327,277	19,782
2025	71	720,256	638,234	2,994

IPP ASSET PROJECTION
FOR A PLAN BEGUN AT AGE 30

		IPP	
Year	Age	Contributions	Fund at year-end
1994	30	12,582	13,046
2000	36	20,418	148,444
2005	41	28,877	363,652
2010	46	41,022	735,568
2015	51	58,456	1,359,885
2020	56	83,486	2,385,929
2025	61	119,419	4,045,229
2030	66	164,208	6,687,753
2035	71[1]	189,400	10,676,964

		RRSP and GIC			
Year	Age	Contributions RRSP	Contributions GIC	RRSP Fund at year end	GIC Fund at year end
1994	30	13,500	(459)	13,997	(467)
2000	36	19,202	608	146,575	993
2005	41	25,096	1,891	345,555	8,323
2010	46	32,799	4,111	672,695	27,000
2015	51	42,868	7,794	1,196,558	66,055
2020	56	56,026	13,730	2,019,483	140,030
2025	61	73,224	23,098	3,293,498	271,929
2030	66	95,701	34,254	5,243,535	494,167
2035	71[1]	125,077	32,162	8,201,241	777,229

(1) IPP advantage over an RRSP at age 71 without considering the GIC Fund: $2,475,723 (30.19%). IPP advantage over an RRSP at age 71 if RRSP contributor has an additional GIC Fund: $1,698,494 (18.92%).

Note that if you overachieve in the extreme, you may decide, in consultation with your actuary, to suspend the IPP plan and return to making full contributions to your RRSP. This flexibility is attractive and, should you have overachieved to the point of ensuring that you will meet your defined benefit if your IPP fund continues to perform well, you will have the comfort of knowing that a good pension is waiting for you at the end of your working days.

As you study the examples you will note that, at 8.5%, you will be 67 years of age before the reduced IPP contributions arising as a result of the surplus will actually be lower than the amount you may have contributed to an RRSP. In the 9.5% example, this will occur for the first time at the age of 58 and for the second time at the age of 61. For this reason, we have included at the bottom of each asset projection a calculation of the IPP advantage both at age 71 and age 66. At 66, most of the impact of surplus is avoided. It is important to keep in mind here that these examples are based on an individual who

IPP BENEFIT PROJECTION
FOR A PLAN BEGUN AT AGE 30

| | | IPP | RRSP and GIC | |
Year	Age	Annual Pension	Annual "Pension" RRSP	Annual "Pension" GIC
2019	55	189,006	161,225	10,735
2025	61	394,571	321,247	26,524
2030	66	729,617	572,056	53,912
2035	71	1,335,225	1,025,619	97,198

began the IPP at age 40. If you began at 35 or 45 or another age, the effects of any surplus (or deficiency for that matter) would occur at a different spot.

So at what age is it attractive to commence an IPP program? Take a look at the projections for a 30 year old (pages 124-5).

Note that, at age 30, the IPP contributions column is $918 lower ($459 lower after the tax deduction is taken into account) than the RRSP contributions column. This is because the amount you can contribute to an IPP is lower the younger you are since a younger individual has more time to accumulate wealth and reach the defined benefit target. And remember, set-up and maintenance costs are not taken into account. These costs reduce the IPP advantage somewhat as we have seen.

But note the huge amount in the IPP fund column at the age of 71 (and the huge amount in the RRSP column, as well). Millions of dollars, $10,676,964 in the IPP fund column for example, are built up as a result of the magic of compound growth, which works more powerfully the younger you begin. Note the IPP annual pension at age 71 from the third column of the IPP benefit projection, $1,335,225—a sizeable annual pension even when discounted for the effects of inflation. Forty-one years of inflation (71 - 30) at 4% would still generate an approximate pension of $250,000 *in today's dollars*, $125,000 after tax according to our assumptions. And that will still be worth almost $5,000 a month (after tax and in today's dollars) at the age of 90.

This demonstrates that my earlier comments about the need for a 40 year old to invest beyond RRSP or IPP contribution limits to achieve financial security don't apply to the same extent to someone who begins earlier, for example at age 30. But they apply even more to someone over 40. The trouble is, most 30 year olds put off accumulating wealth until later. Imagine the possibilities if you began at 20 or 25!

But nevertheless, it's obvious from the IPP projections above that 30 is too early an age to begin an IPP. The RRSP is simply better at that age—and you do want the best. As indicated earlier, the ideal age is in the late 30s or even a little older, depending on set-up and maintenance costs. Certainly, the older you are the more immediate tax savings you will realize as a result of higher IPP contribution levels.

For your information and convenience, IPP projections calculated for plans begun at five year intervals from ages 30 to 65 are reproduced in Appendix II.

So why aren't IPPs better known? Why don't we hear more about them? The question I get asked frequently is why the individual's accountant or financial adviser has not brought the IPP to his or her attention.

First, executive pension planning is more complex than the RRSP. A pension plan must be drafted and accepted by the government for registration. In the case of the IPP, a trust settlement must be prepared and executed to establish the pension trust fund. The defined benefit for the pension plan must be calculated and an opinion rendered by a qualified actuary. Filings with the government must be made annually and there must be periodic actuarial valuations. The RRSP, on the other hand, is a savings plan. Once the savings plan is established, it's merely a matter of making the allowable contributions.

The IPP, however, is not as complex as it might appear at first blush. Those who practice in the area of executive pension planning and deferred compensation (a limited number of lawyers, accountants, actuaries and pension consultants) can deal directly and quickly with the steps necessary to establish an IPP.

Second, the IPP, while it may be of benefit in some circumstances to those with salaries well below the high five-figure to low six-figure range, is most effective and powerful for those on higher incomes. This excludes many working Canadians. In each case a cost-benefit analysis must be undertaken to determine the extent to which an IPP could be beneficial.

It's difficult, therefore, for those in the financial planning sector to justify marketing the IPP as a product. It isn't simply a matter of running advertisements and hiring one or more individuals to receive contributions. In any event, the market may not be large enough to justify the venture.

Third, it must be noted that it is not possible to establish a spousal IPP. The spousal RRSP has become a popular income splitting device, and the theory is that it will enable the spouses to plan to have equal incomes on retirement. Presumably, at the time of retirement the income levels will be lower and both spouses might therefore be in the middle or lowest tax bracket by having split their retirement income in this way.

This warrants two comments. First, since the RRSP is generally retained to some extent as an additional tax sheltering device notwithstanding the existence of the IPP, it might be appropriate to place all the RRSP funds spousally to the degree possible to counterbalance in part the non-spousal nature of the IPP. Second, other investments may be organized spousally if income splitting is a feature of the overall tax planning strategy of the spouses.

In summary, I believe that, for those Canadians with sufficient earned income, the IPP is a very attractive tax sheltering device. And most if not all of the common objections to it arise from a lack of information and understanding of either the IPP or the process of accumulating wealth. As more and more Canadians incorporate companies of their own, I predict that the IPP will become the planning tool of choice in the future. As it becomes better known among Canadian executives, highly paid employees, business people and professionals, they will turn to the IPP to provide the best possible pension plan.

In this age of the computer chip, an IPP asset/benefit analysis can be run for any individual in Canada based on his or her date of birth and income, taking into account set-up costs, maintenance costs, the effect of GST (if any) and anticipated rates of return, whether above or below the 7.5% currently prescribed by pension law. Armed with this information, an intelligent decision can be made.

One final note on one of the most important financial planning issues that arises, both in the context of the IPP and the RRSP, that of postponing withdrawal from the tax sheltered pool of investment funds for as long as possible to enable the maximum tax sheltered compounded growth to occur. While you can contribute to an IPP or RRSP to the age of 71 if you have the earned income to support it, most of you, I realize, would prefer to stop working sooner than that, perhaps in your mid-to-late 50s or early 60s.

Through proper financial planning it is generally possible to establish yet another fund, preferably tax sheltered, to provide a bridging or interim pension or pool of capital to delay taking funds from the IPP or RRSP too early. After getting all of that tax sheltered money in there it would be a shame to take it out if it could double once or twice more. It's the last doubling that makes the big difference, especially if attractive rates of return are achieved on your IPP or RRSP investments. One additional device that may be used to accomplish this bridging or transition is exempt life insurance.

Exempt Life Insurance

Exempt life insurance is a tax sheltering tool that can facilitate wealth accumulation if approached properly. To quote Coopers & Lybrand, 1991:

> "Those looking for tax shelters... may wish to explore the benefits that may be derived from an "exempt" life insurance policy, ... a powerful tool in the tax planning arsenal..."

They make a good point, and exempt life insurance is especially effective if used in conjunction with an overall tax planning and tax sheltering strategy. So what is exempt life insurance? First, it is life insurance. A certain amount of life insurance is purchased. Premiums may be paid monthly and, at the end of the day, a certain cash value will be built up.

Although the premiums will generally be higher in the early years than if term insurance were purchased, term life insurance premiums have the nasty habit of rising as you get older, to significant levels. When compared over the life of the policy, the total cost of the insurance component of exempt life insurance may be approximately equal to the cost of term insurance, excluding the cash surrender value of the policy, something pure term insurance does not have.

Some in the financial planning industry maintain that term insurance is the better buy in most cases because the initial premiums are lower. If you were to invest on your own accord the extra amounts that would have been required as premiums in a policy with a cash surrender value, greater wealth could be created, even in a fully taxable environment, than the amount that would build up in cash surrender value.

While this is true, most of us don't have the discipline required to invest the difference in the amount of premiums in the early years and this lack of discipline undermines the comparison. But the major advantage of exempt life insurance is another, more significant feature, namely that additional funds can be contributed along with the regular insurance premiums into a tax sheltered pool commonly referred to as a cash accumulation fund.

The basic idea is that you can place an extra amount in the cash accumulation fund as you pay the premiums for the insurance. The more insurance you buy and the higher the premium you pay, the greater the contributions you can make to this fund. I don't want to oversimplify the matter but, solely for the purposes of this discussion, let's assume that for every dollar paid in premiums an additional dollar is contributed to the cash accumulation fund. The fund is invested by the insurance company and a return is paid, which is added on an ongoing basis to the tax sheltered pool of cash. The return may be at or near the rate of return paid on one year GICs.

The power of the cash accumulation fund comes from the fact that its growth is tax sheltered. Meanwhile, the basic premiums provide life insurance on the life of the insured and a cash surrender value.

Contributions made to the cash accumulation fund, unlike those to an RRSP or IPP, are not tax deductible when made. Exempt life insurance is therefore not an immediate tax savings device. Rather, it is a tax deferral device to the extent that monies are contributed in addition to the basic insurance premiums and they can grow inside the fund in a tax advantaged way.

The rate of return on the monies in the cash accumulation fund is determined by the insured's agreement with the insurance company. True, the rates are not astronomical. But as we have seen, the power of tax sheltered growth can, depending on the amount of insurance purchased, generate a substantial pool of money over the years, another example of tax sheltered compounding. Remember, for those of you in the 50% tax bracket, a tax sheltered rate of return of, say, 8% is really the same as twice that much, 16%, in a fully taxed environment.

The cash accumulation fund of an exempt life insurance policy may then be used as a bridge, another pool of capital to draw on in retirement, enabling you to delay withdrawing money from your RRSP or IPP. Remember that money invested in an RRSP or IPP also doubles in a tax sheltered environment and that, with proper planning, you should have a significant amount built up in one or both of these sheltered vehicles. What a shame, therefore, to withdraw money from an RRSP or IPP earlier than necessary, particularly if you are earning excellent rates of return by employing wise investment strategies. Would it not be appropriate to plan your affairs to enable the RRSP or IPP value to continue to grow and double a while longer?

Take this example. Assume you had $500,000 in your RRSP or IPP. Assume that the rate of return you're achieving is 12% and that, applying the Rule of 72s, this $500,000 tax sheltered fund would double yet again to approximately $1,000,000 in six more years (72 ÷ 12 = 6). Assume that you have also built up several hundred thousand dollars in an exempt insurance cash accumulation fund over the years. Would it not be possible to draw on or borrow against your cash accumulation fund for several years, perhaps as many as six years, to leave your substantial RRSP or IPP pool to increase or perhaps double one more time before touching it? Depending on your age and all of the surrounding circumstances, this approach is possible and is an example of using exempt life insurance as a bridging tool to get the most out of your RRSP or IPP.

Although tax sheltering devices are few in number in Canada, they are particularly powerful. Foremost among these are the RRSP and the IPP.

Delaying the withdrawal of RRSP or IPP funds with the help of the bridging capability of exempt life insurance or some other pool of assets will allow you to build a substantial tax sheltered pool for retirement purposes.

The next challenge is to achieve healthy returns so that your tax sheltered funds may double as many times as possible. As we have seen, the results of such tax sheltered compounding can be incredible. The key to accomplishing this is the employment of intelligent, low risk investment strategies, the subject of the next chapter.

6

PUTTING YOUR CAPITAL TO WORK

I T IS NOT ENOUGH TO FREE UP CASH and place funds in a
tax sheltered environment. Those sheltered resources must
be working for you to generate the most wealth possible,
wealth that will outstrip the impact of taxes and inflation,
those two wealth destroyers.

SETTING OBJECTIVES

The first step in putting your capital to work is to ascertain
precisely why you are doing so—in other words, setting your

135

objectives, setting goals. Where do you want to be in 10 years, 20 years, 30 years? When do you want to retire? What sort of lifestyle do you hope to have? Do you have a dream to "retire" to that second career or avocation you've never had the time to pursue, such as getting to that novel that's waiting to be written? Mine is to return to the stage as a concert pianist, the career of my 20s, something I pursue today only occasionally in aid of charitable causes. Whatever it is, you need an objective to strive for. How likely is it that you will get where you want to go or have the resources to pursue your goals if you don't know exactly where you're headed?

Since your dreams are personal to you and your family and since the degree of wealth you'll need to realize those dreams will vary depending on your personal situation, what follows is theoretical only, a framework for you to use to undertake your own analysis.

The simplest way to begin your calculations is to work with a few basic facts, your current age (which, for the following example, I will assume to be 40), your anticipated retirement age (I will assume 65), your life expectancy (I will assume 90), inflation (4%), taxes (zero now in a tax sheltered environment and 50% *of each and every dollar* many years down the road, to allow for anticipated tax increases by the time your retirement monies are withdrawn), and an income in the 90th year (after the 50% tax) of $3,000 a month *in today's dollars with today's buying power*. Let's assume that I am the person in this example and that I will achieve a 12% annual rate of return throughout.

I have 25 years left to work. I will live 25 years beyond retirement age. The question is, how much must I set aside monthly, starting now, to achieve my objective of $3,000 a month after tax in my 90th year?

I start by working backwards from my 90th year. I will need $6,000 a month before tax to have $3,000 a month after tax. That's $72,000 a year gross income, which in turn is a 12% return on my savings. My savings at that time, therefore, must be $600,000 ($600,000 x 12% = $72,000).

But since I won't have any new savings after I retire at 65, how much will I need in savings at 65 to account for inflation throughout my 25 retirement years? In other words, how many dollars at age 65 equal $600,000 25 years later if inflation averages 4%? The answer is $1,700,000 approximately. This amount at age 65 will dwindle in its buying power by age 90 to $600,000 as a result of the impact of inflation. But this $1,700,000 is in dollars valued 25 years from now. So how much money is needed in total to allow as well for that additional 25 years of inflation? The answer is $4,700,000.

So, I need $4,700,000 built up in the next 25 years! At first blush, it sounds impossible. Can I do it? How much a month must I set aside, starting *now*? The answer is approximately $2,500 a month, $600 a week, $30,000 a year, $85 a day! Approximately or exactly, who cares? It's an awful lot. I can't afford it. I don't have $2,500 a month to set aside. Do you? Our friend Harry Dentist from the prologue of this book does, but he is just beginning to realize it. But are dentists and others with similar income levels the only ones in a position to be financially secure if they live to a ripe old age?

No. Before you get all discouraged and throw your dreams (and this book) away, a whole series of additional factors must also be considered to get a realistic picture. The purpose of the example above was to give you a frame of reference and to take a first step—a large one, I admit—in acquiring a wealth accumulation mindset.

First, if $4,700,000 accumulated over the next 25 years is enough to provide me with an adequate after tax income when I'm 90, it must be more than enough at age 65. In fact, my retirement income, in today's dollars, at age 65 will be $17,000 a month before tax and $8,500 a month after tax. In other words, $8,500 a month at age 65 equals the buying power of $3,000 a month at age 90.

If I have $8,500 a month to live on at age 65, won't I be able to save some and invest those savings and continue my wealth accumulation program into my retirement years? Or, to put it another way, couldn't I set aside less than $2,500 a month now and still get where I want to go? The answer is yes. How much less depends, as well, on some or all of the factors discussed below.

Second, to the extent that I contribute to an RRSP, the government will, in effect, pay half of the cost if I am in the 50% tax bracket or 40% if I am in the middle bracket, by way of income tax savings. This will cut the cost of my wealth accumulation program substantially if I reinvest those savings.

Third, I have ignored in my example the possibility of encroaching on capital, that is to say dipping into my pool of accumulated wealth in the later years. The pension analyses for IPPs and RRSPs in Chapter 5 assume, you will recall, that I will exhaust my capital in those vehicles by the time I get to the end of my lifespan based on the life expectancy for a Canadian male. In my example I have assumed that all of the funds I accumulate will be there for my estate on my death, that I will have lived solely on the interest from my investments and will not have touched a penny of the capital. While leaving a plump estate on death may be attractive, it's not necessary to leave it all. I could dip into the funds for my own benefit.

Fourth, I have ignored as well the possibility of buying an annuity on retirement. An annuity is a product sold by life insurance companies whereby I invest my savings and am guaranteed an amount of income by the insurance company for as long as I live. There are many types of annuities, some with survivor benefits for a surviving spouse, some indexed for inflation, some with guarantee periods so that, should I die prematurely, my estate might receive a benefit. The price and features of annuities vary considerably and purchasers should shop carefully and weigh all of the factors.

Then there is the possibility of acquiring a Registered Retirement Income Fund (RRIF), which generally could be arranged with a financial institution to provide an annual income from my savings to the age of 90 (and my spouse to the age of 90) with my savings remaining under my control rather than under the control of an insurance company. And, in the context of the IPP, there is the option of actually taking the pension, the defined benefit, which would be payable based on my life expectancy. You will recall the discussion in Chapter 5 concerning the pension for a surviving spouse and the fact that undepleted capital can go into the estate.

Annuities, RRIFs and IPP pensions can make a dramatic impact on my example, generally with the effect of providing retirement income without the need for as great a pool of funds as we first calculated.

Fifth, my example does not make allowance for any Canada Pension Plan or Old Age Security (although I repeat my caution that these may not exist a decade or two down the road, at least in their present form, or may be clawed back from those of us who have accumulated substantial wealth by our own devices).

But do not allow these five factors to lull you into any false sense of security. My example also assumes that all of my savings and the growth on those savings will be 100% tax sheltered, which may or may not be your case, depending on circumstances.

And I have assumed a consistent rate of return of 12% per year over a 50 year period. I can tell you that, while many have exceeded this rate of return consistently in recent years despite rather low interest rates, it's not necessarily easy to do. Recall the discussion in Chapter 3 about the dramatic impact of just a few percentage points of interest earned. For example, the $2,500 a month savings needed in my example would be increased to approximately $4,200 a month if I achieved only 9% return, but would be reduced to approximately $1,500 a month if I achieved 15%.

As you can see, there are many factors, so it's impossible to give you a single, magic number for your monthly savings. It depends on your age, the factors above (and no doubt other factors as well) and your personal dreams and ambitions. My objective in this discussion will have been fulfilled if you begin calculating based on your own circumstances. I spent hour after hour some time back doing just that for myself and my family. I actually enjoyed the exercise. I hope you do too.

Finding Good Advice

The first step in achieving your financial objectives is to seek out good financial advice. The second challenge is to know how to recognize it when you find it. The third is to act on it.

None of this is as easy to do as it may sound. Again, remember our friend the dentist from the prologue. He was getting advice from all sides, from his accountant, a financial adviser, a real estate agent, an insurance agent, a tax lawyer and an endless stream of salespeople converging at his office door. If we delved a little further we would no doubt also uncover his banker, his colleagues, his brother-in-law and the postman, to mention a few.

Yes, financial advice is easy enough to find. In fact, it is quite difficult to avoid. But is any of it any good? Undoubtedly, some of it is, but which bits? And remember, you are an individual with unique circumstances and your own personality and objectives. A bit of advice that is good for another person may not be good for you.

Ideally, therefore, you are or will soon become an expert in all of the things we're discussing and will be able to navigate your own financial course to your personal financial objectives. No one knows you and your objectives or cares more about them than you do.

But not all of us have the inclination or the time or the expertise to look after our own financial affairs. You may fall into this group, and if you do you'll need to seek out the expertise you require. What should you look for and where should you look for it?

You should look for assistance, but not for someone to take complete charge of your financial affairs. You must stay in charge. However attractive and desirable it may appear to be to abdicate responsibility, you have a role to play. If I may compare your financial life to a ship, you and you alone must be the captain. No one else can really control it for you and no one else should. That doesn't mean you can't have a first mate and, for that matter, a crew. But you must stay at the helm even if your decisions, especially the earlier ones, come primarily from advice from your fellow sailors.

Professional assistance should be sought at two levels. The first is structural and concerns tax planning. You must get your basic structures (corporations, trusts and the like) organized properly to reduce the tax you pay to the legal minimum.

Ideally you will engage the services of a tax planning lawyer or tax planning accountant. Be careful here. You need someone who is really into tax planning, someone who can look at your financial position and objectives and then as creatively as possible assemble the structures to assist you in getting where you want to go. This is not cookie-cutter work where all you need is this structure or that structure. You need tax tools designed with your personal objectives in mind. Nothing less will do.

The best way to assess a potential tax planning lawyer or tax planning accountant is first to determine whether his or her practice really is oriented to tax planning matters. Ask around, and question the lawyer or accountant about the nature of the practice. What sort of clients does he or she assist, and how?

Perhaps the most telltale way to get to the bottom of it is to ask how your prospective adviser might go about helping you. He or she might suggest a cursory look at your tax returns to see what could be done. Expect to be asked for personal and business financial statements as well as for a statement of your objectives, your goals. And expect to be questioned about your financial affairs. In other words, is this person really interested in planning and crafting your tax plan as part of an overall picture? If not, you're in the wrong place.

Please note that many people confuse the roles of accountant and tax accountant. They are generally two different things. An accountant may be a tax accountant, but this is usually not the case. Where the confusion comes from is the fact that most accountants prepare tax returns. Many people, accountants and non-accountants, prepare tax returns. This does not necessarily render them tax planners.

The situation, particularly with business people and professionals, who are more likely to use the services of an accountant at least for tax return preparation, is further complicated by the fact that for such people the accountant is often the closest professional outside their own field of endeavour with whom they work on a regular (or at least annual) basis. Therefore, it seems logical to run tax planning ideas, investment ideas and the like past the accountant for a second opinion.

With all due respect to the accounting profession and the importance of its role—and I'm fully aware of the fact that the problem often begins with the client's misunderstanding of the accountant's role—I must say that many good tax planning and financial planning ideas die in the accountant's office. (In fairness, I must add that a lot of bad ideas die there too.) Why is this?

The truth be known, accountants are by nature rather conservative. To give the green light to a new idea or approach is not the conservative thing to do. Why not stick to the tried and true? And if the new idea fails, won't the client blame the accountant for not having spoken out against it? Actually, in this context you are putting the accountant in a tough spot by asking.

In the tax planning context it's even worse for the accountant than in the context of financial planning. The accountant is preparing your annual tax return. You suspect or someone tells you that you are paying too much tax. A solution is proposed and you run it by your accountant. If the accountant approves it and it doesn't work, the accountant may fear he or she will be blamed. If it does work, the accountant may fear that he or she will be blamed for not recommending it years earlier or at least being knowledgeable enough to refer you to someone who could help you. It's a classic lose-lose situation, or could be perceived that way. The safer response, therefore, is to reject the tax planning proposal. In fairness, many accountants ignore the perceived risk and work with the client and the client's tax planner. And in that event, in my experience, everyone wins, including the accountant whose client grows by virtue of setting out on the road to wealth accumulation.

My advice regarding the use of accountants, therefore, is to try to understand their role—preparing tax returns and financial statements, audits and the like—and to engage them as a member of your team as appropriate. Ask for their advice, of course, but understand where that advice fits into your overall approach.

Once you have looked after your tax plan, you are ready to move to the second level, financial planning. This requires building a financial planning team. I recommend that you look first for that first mate we discussed, someone to manage the crew. We call this person a financial planner.

Now, the problem with the term "financial planner" is that it has no legal definition in most jurisdictions and therefore the use of the term is largely unregulated. What you're looking for is a person of broad experience, a team leader, someone interested in your long-term financial welfare, someone who sees the big picture with you in it.

This person might hold a licence to sell financial products of certain types and might double as the team member responsible for this aspect of your wealth accumulation program. Your concern here is that the financial planner not put his or her interest in commissions from the sale of these products ahead of your interests. There is a possible conflict of interest here. Watch out for it.

Some financial planners sell no financial products, preferring instead to bill for their time on an hourly basis. Frequently, it is possible to pay for an initial consultation and, if you are sufficiently impressed, to retain the financial planner to prepare a written proposal for you with suggestions about how you might proceed to build a team and pursue your objectives. Personally, I prefer this approach to that of engaging a financial planner who is also a salesperson.

In my experience, the best way to select a financial planner is a combination of word of mouth references and interviewing the candidate for the position yourself. Then make your selection.

Now, under your personal supervision, the financial planner should help you refine your personal financial plan, one that accords with your personal tax plan. Then you should determine what sort of financial team members you'll need to effect it. Presumably this will include at least a banker, a stock broker and an insurance agent.

As for bankers, they can finance transactions where required, provide banking references, maintain accounts and perform similar banking functions. Remember, they are generally not financial planners. They are also generally very conservative; it's the nature of their business. But like your accountant, your banker is part of your team and has a role to play.

And, with the recent reform of the federal laws relating to financial institutions, that role is expanding to include trust and financial services. I suggest you enquire both at your bank and at trust companies about the range of services offered. Banks and trust companies are bound to become more competitive in coming years as they vie for the retirement dollars of our aging population.

Next, stockbrokers. It is difficult (but by no means impossible) to find a good stockbroker, especially when you're in the early stages of your wealth accumulation program and don't have an impressive amount of money to invest. You don't want a broker who will abuse you by dumping securities on you that their more important clients are advised to unload. You don't want someone who ignores you, who acquires a security for you and then fails to keep close tabs on it or forgets you when something juicy is transpiring. You don't want someone who will "churn" your account. Churning is the process of selling one security and purchasing another primarily so that the broker earns a commission. Churning generally benefits the broker but not you.

So just how do you find a good stockbroker? Being a good stockbroker requires knowledge, nerve, judgement and, assuming those three, discipline. Lack of discipline is the easiest to spot. Put yourself in the broker's position for a moment: hundreds of clients, thousands of trades, a constant stream of changing data. It's easy to get swamped, difficult to keep on top of it. The key is organization, discipline. Switch brokers if yours is sluggish, can't respond quickly, or doesn't appear to be on top of your file. I'm afraid a little trial and error will be necessary here. But begin by meeting the broker face to face to explore your objectives and expectations.

In the case of the insurance agent, you're looking for someone from a firm that is well established and financially secure. A firm with a top credit rating would be appropriate. Ask about that.

As for the individual agent, you want someone with an understanding of exempt life insurance (see Chapter 5) and the insurance aspects of estate planning (see Chapter 8). Nothing less will do, so ask questions about those two areas. Does the agent recommend exempt insurance? Why? What are the agent's views on insurance in the context of estate planning? You want to determine whether the agent sees insurance in the larger picture of your personal wealth accumulation plan.

In any event, begin today to build a wealth accumulation crew. Get your tax planning in order and set your crew to work on achieving your goals.

TYPES OF INVESTMENT

This book aims to convey a philosophy for accumulating wealth rather than a mass of detail and information about specific investments. For the latter the reader is referred to a wide range of good publications, available in bookstores across Canada, on various investment vehicles and opportunities. The books of Gordon Pape stand out in particular as sensible, informed writing on a range of investment subjects. But first an overview of a basic approach to low risk investing.

Risk   The words "low risk" are the key. If inflation averages 4% (or anywhere in the 2% to 4% range) we want average returns of 12%, eight to 10 percentage points above the average rate of inflation, or even better if we can get it. This eight to 10 point spread will ensure that you outrun not only inflation but taxes to the extent that your investments are not tax sheltered. To the extent that they are—and hopefully a sizeable chunk is—this spread will facilitate healthy compound growth as we saw in Chapters 4 and 5. This will enable you to accumulate substantial wealth over time. Anything less is certainly a risk, the risk that you won't accumulate sufficient wealth to achieve your financial objectives.

But there's more to risk than that. The return (reward) you receive for making a particular investment—whether in the form of interest, dividends or capital gains—is generally in direct relationship to the degree of risk you take. If you take a huge risk—for example, you buy a speculative penny stock at 10 cents and it goes to 60 cents the next day and you sell— you'll have made 600% in one day. But the odds are that it won't go to 60 cents or anywhere like that. In fact, more likely than not it will go nowhere or go down, perhaps to zero. If it went to 2 cents the next week, your loss would be 80% in one week.

If, on the other hand, you purchase an interest bearing instrument such as a one year Guaranteed Investment Certificate (GIC) paying 6% per year, you know what you will get: 6% growth (ignoring taxes and inflation). In one sense this is virtually a no risk investment, at least assuming it's covered by deposit insurance.

For those of you who don't know what deposit insurance is, it's up to $60,000 of insurance provided by the Canada

Deposit Insurance Corporation (CDIC), a Crown corporation that insures certain types of deposits and investments with certain financial institutions in case the institutions go belly-up. Watch for it. When making deposits or investments with financial institutions, ask for a copy of any CDIC literature about the deposit insurance as it applies to your deposit or investment. Spread your deposits or investments around to avoid exceeding the $60,000 insurance limit. Remember, deposit insurance doesn't apply to all deposits and investments. Ask, and then double-check by phoning the CDIC deposit insurance hotline at 1-800-461-2342.

Returning to our GIC paying 6% per year, the return is too low. And, in further recognition of the lack of risk you are taking, the government will take 50% of every dollar you earn on your GIC if you hold it outside a tax sheltered environment and are in the 50% tax bracket.

Does this mean, then, that you should avoid interest bearing instruments such as GICs? No, they still have a place in your investment portfolio. First, longer-term GICs generally pay better returns than shorter-term ones. Some financial institutions pay better rates than others. Shop around. Second, put interest bearing instruments such as GICs inside your RRSP or other tax sheltered vehicles. You will defer taxation that way and only have inflation to worry about.

And use interest bearing instruments as a hedge against your riskier investments. If an investment with a higher risk and higher potential for return lets you down, at least your good old GIC (or whatever) will be chugging along in your favour. In other words, balance your risk to some extent between investments with greater risk (still, low risk in the main, please) and sure things such as GICs.

Types of Investment Income   To explore the idea of low risk investing further, it is essential to distinguish between investments that generate capital gains, dividends and interest income. You will recall from Chapter 4 that you get no tax break on interest income, whereas dividend income is subject to the dividend tax credit and capital gains are taxed on only 75% of the gain at this time, subject also to the capital gains exemption.

This means that, to the extent you have some investment inside tax sheltered vehicles and some outside (as will most likely be the case as you travel further down the road to wealth accumulation), you should ensure that it is the tax advantaged investments, those that generate dividends and capital gains—particularly if you have not used the capital gains exemption as yet—that sit outside the tax sheltered environment. They will attract less tax and therefore enable you to accumulate more wealth.

Dividends are paid to those who hold stocks in corporations and certain mutual funds. Corporate profits are, in whole or in part (at the discretion of the board of directors of a corporation), distributed to the shareholders in the form of dividends. Capital gains, as we saw in Chapter 4, can arise from the sale of capital property (including land and corporate stocks) at a profit.

With that introduction, it is now appropriate to make a few brief comments on certain common investments available to you in the Canadian investment marketplace.

Real Estate

Although this comment may offend the sensibilities of some, it is my view that, with localized exceptions, real estate will not be the investment in the next 30 years that it has been in the last 30. I recognize the old adage: buy land because they aren't making any more of it. After all, Harry Dentist did. But what's happened to that land since he bought it? There is a core of truth to the statement about the limited supply of land, but in most parts of Canada significant population increase does not appear to be in the offing. It also does not appear that traditional factories surrounded by suburbs full of youthful factory workers and middle managers are in the cards either.

The Great Restructuring—from large manufacturers to small corporations able to add value in an information-based economy—will take pressure off our big cities as the ability to do business on a national and international basis spreads across the regions of this country. The new economic order means that there will be less and less concentration of economic development of the sort that spawned the real estate booms in Canadian cities. With few exceptions, the next few decades will be an era of fragmentation of economic development. Hence, it is my view that parking money in moose pasture will not necessarily be the way to secure high rates of return.

Stocks

What about the stock market? The key is to have a good stockbroker, as we discussed earlier in this chapter. I must admit that I have tried dabbling on my own, with spotty results. I just did not have the hands-on knowledge and the access to information necessary to make informed decisions quickly. I didn't know when to buy and I didn't know when to sell. Knowledge and timing are everything in the market.

The other thing I lacked at the outset was enough money for a stockbroker to diversify my portfolio. How does one diversify a few thousand dollars? At that level, it is only possible to buy into a few stocks, putting your eggs in a very few baskets. This is risky. I should have avoided buying specific stocks at this juncture. My advice, therefore, is avoid putting all of your money in one or two stocks. Avoid putting any significant percentage of your portfolio into penny stocks and new, unproven issues. Diversify. Spread the risk around according to your particular investment philosophy and tolerance of risk.

GICs, Treasury Bills and Bonds

Then there are interest bearing instruments, which include GICs and T-bills (treasury bills). Many investors perceive these to be safer than stocks and mutual funds. This is because interest bearing instruments generally pay a specified rate of return in the form of interest.

GICs are offered by financial institutions and come in all shapes and sizes. GICs are purchased for a fixed length of time (one year, five years or whatever) and pay a guaranteed rate of return for that period. They generally cannot be cashed until they mature. If you require liquidity or are otherwise parking your money awaiting other investment opportunities, consider other investment instruments offered by your financial institution, including term deposits or so-called money market funds.

T-bills are government instruments offered by the government to generate cash from the private sector. These can usually be purchased through your financial institution and the rate of interest paid depends on market forces. Your financial institution will be pleased to quote you the prevailing T-bill rate as compared with GICs, term deposits and other products it offers.

As we have seen, however, the challenge when acquiring interest bearing instruments is to obtain a rate of return high enough to accumulate wealth in the face of taxes and inflation.

Bonds are another common investment, and it is important to understand how bonds work. The face value or price at which bonds may be bought or sold generally changes with the current interest rate. Bonds with a high rate of interest attached to them will be sold at a premium during periods when prevailing interest rates are low; they will be discounted if current rates are higher. Make sure that you have a thorough understanding of the relationship between interest rates and face value before venturing into the bond market. Your financial planner and your broker should be of assistance here. They will be aware of various bond issues and how they are performing or are likely to perform.

Note that it is considered attractive to buy bonds (or mutual funds that invest in bonds) when interest rates are high and on the decline but not when interest rates are rising. It is considered wise to buy other interest bearing instruments when rates are high and generally on the rise. When rates are low and appear to be at or near the bottom, most advisers will suggest a switch to equities, whether in the form of stocks or through mutual funds that invest in equities. This is because the equity markets generally outperform other forms of investments when interest rates are low. Hence the stampede to mutual funds in the early 1990s.

Mutual Funds

The most popular item on the market today is mutual funds. Mutual funds are all the rage primarily because interest rates are relatively low and certain funds or families of funds have performed exceedingly well. The real question is whether past performance is any indication of future performance. These funds go in cycles with stronger and weaker periods.

Basically, a mutual fund embodies the concepts of spreading risk among a range of investments and combining the purchasing power of a number of investors. Those who purchase shares in a mutual fund place their money in a common pool, and the mutual fund manager invests the money from the pool in a wide range of investments, thereby spreading the risk across that range.

Certain mutual fund managers determine that they will invest only in stocks, others in bonds, others in interest bearing instruments and so forth. Other funds invest in more than one type of investment vehicle but have different goals: income generation, capital growth and so on. Some pay dividends. The combinations and permutations are virtually endless, and hundreds and hundreds of mutual funds, both domestic and international, have sprung up over the past few decades.

My advice concerning mutual funds is as follows. First, I like mutual funds. Try them. They can get you that 12% or more you are seeking. Second, past performance is not necessarily an indication of future performance. Why does performance in the fund fluctuate? How does the volatility of the fund—the stability of its monthly rate of return, preferably over the past 60 months—compare with the volatility of similar funds? Third, any particular mutual fund is only as good as the mutual fund managers. Obtain a copy of the mutual fund prospectus by calling the mutual fund directly. Pay particular attention to the mutual fund's management team and especially to any changes that may occur in it. How experienced are they? How long have they been there? What results have they achieved? Fourth, while it is not advisable to ride a bad investment all the way into the ground, even in the case of a mutual fund, do not be overly hasty to withdraw, particularly if there are fees to be paid on leaving one mutual fund and joining another. Remember, mutual fund shares go up and down. You don't want to panic and sell every time they go down a bit. It's the overall growth over a year or number of years that you are looking for. But be prepared to switch if the fund just isn't performing as well as certain others.

In that regard, note that certain mutual funds are "no load," which generally means that there is no fee to join or leave the fund or to switch from one fund to another within the same mutual fund family. Whether a mutual fund is truly no load can be determined by reading the prospectus, the information document the law requires be given to you before you purchase publicly traded securities. Read that document very carefully. Don't just skim it. You owe it to yourself to be informed.

To summarize, I recommend that you find a good financial planner, build a team of financial advisers and work closely with your financial advisers on the understanding that it is your responsibility to be informed, keep in touch and make the ultimate decisions. You're the one who must live with the consequences.

And keep your objective in mind: to earn at least 12% (or, more precisely, 8% to 10% over the prevailing rate of inflation) per annum on average. Assess returns annually and be prepared to take action. Do not be satisfied with single digit rates of return, as real wealth cannot normally be accumulated that way.

In the final analysis, however, it is not the financial planner, stockbroker, banker, accountant or lawyer who must decide your financial future. The ultimate responsibility rests where it should, at your own doorstep.

The purpose of this book is to provide a framework, a philosophy for accumulating wealth, one that includes freeing up capital by good tax planning and approaches such as the 10% solution and then placing those savings, to the maximum extent possible, in a tax sheltered environment to compound into substantial wealth over the years ahead. Ultimately, therefore, it is you who must understand this and ensure that it happens. It's your money, your future.

PART
III

Managing Wealth –
Coping with Success

7

TAKING ON THE WORLD

O
NCE YOU HAVE ORGANIZED YOUR AFFAIRS to free up
capital, including saving taxes to the extent legally
permissible, and invested that capital in tax sheltered
vehicles such as RRSPs and IPPs, you will be well on your
way to generating substantial wealth. It will be built over
time, assuming the rates of return on your investment arc sufficient to overcome the effects of inflation, however high or
low inflation may be from time to time.

Presumably you will also have taken advantage of the small
business deduction and capital gains exemption (both discussed in Chapter 4) and put in place a program to reduce

non-deductible debt. In the early years of your wealth accumulation program, doing all of this will probably have the
effect of utilizing every bit (and more) of any version of the
10% solution you decide to implement (also Chapter 4).

But is that the end of the story? The economy, and investment opportunities, encompass the globe. Should a Canadian
investor consider developing an international investment
strategy? There is no reason not to and the rationale is clear.

Global Investment Opportunities

Canadians have always invested both inside and outside
Canada's borders and global investment has been on the
increase in recent years. While there are those who believe
that investment should stay at home (and that foreign investment in Canada should be discouraged), I generally disagree.
While a country should own the engines of its economic
growth, and prosperity and national borders and domestic
economic policy remain important, if Canadian capital is
encouraged to participate in the global arena, there will be
benefits to both Canada and the individual investor. In fact, it
is unlikely that prosperity at the individual or national level
will be assured if we isolate ourselves.

Extending my earlier thesis that prosperity will best be
achieved if capital is employed in the most effective way possible, I believe that the same rationale opens the door to international investment. As much money as possible should be
free to find the most productive place it can, the place where
the best possible rates of return can be achieved. These returns
are often available inside Canada. This is especially true in the
context of tax sheltered vehicles such as RRSPs and IPPs

because one of the two major wealth destroyers, income tax, is deferred when investments are placed inside these vehicles. However, once you have utilized domestic tax sheltered vehicles to the maximum, you should consider investing globally.

There are capitalist economies in every part of the world and any number of international investment opportunities. Furthermore, since all domestic economies go through cycles of growth and recession, at any given time some economies are in decline or transition (as must be said to be the case in Canada right now) and others are experiencing unparalleled growth.

COMPARATIVE STOCK MARKET PERFORMANCE MID–1992

Netherlands 20%
Belgium 16%
Mexico 19%
United States 5%
France 17%
Canada 8%

The preceding table is a snapshot of selected equity markets taken in the middle of 1992. At that particular point in the year, Canadian markets were down approximately 8%, although they did recover by the end of 1992 to reflect a 2% rate of growth on average and improved further in 1993. But look at some of the other countries and how their markets were performing at the same time.

Then look at the table opposite on page 163, which highlights the change between 1981 and 1991 in the world equity markets, that is, where the world's capital is invested. In 1981, more than half (56%) was invested in the United States and Canada. By 1991, largely due to the rise in value of the equity markets of the Pacific Basin, the investment in Canada and the United States had declined to 39% of the world total—a substantial drop. And the trend is continuing. In a shrinking world, with computers, faxes, satellites and the like, it is increasingly easy to invest globally and take advantage of such trends.

The traditional investment advice given by investment advisers in Canada has been to keep most or all of your investments here at home. Perhaps this advice came not so much because the professional adviser did not believe in taking advantage of international opportunities as because the Canadian investor has not traditionally been a global thinker. Most advisers realize there is no point in giving global advice to a person with a domestic mindset.

But all of this is changing. Increasingly, financial advisers are recommending a global investment strategy, and Canadians are becoming more and more receptive to the idea. Our need for higher and higher returns in the face of higher

World Equity Market Capitalization

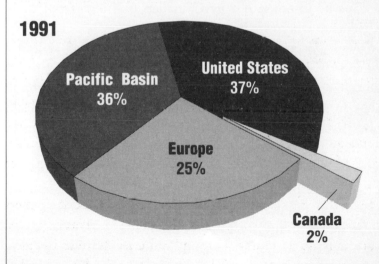

1981

United States
51%

Pacific Basin
22%

Europe
22%

Canada
5%

1991

Pacific Basin
36%

United States
37%

Europe
25%

Canada
2%

and higher taxes may be spurring the change as well as an increased awareness that the world does not end at the Canadian border. Once you've become accustomed to domestic investment and benefited from all the opportunities it offers, it's time to think about expanding your horizons.

Another point to consider is that an increasing number of Canadians now appreciate that the Canadian dollar is not necessarily the only currency in which to hold investments. How stable will it be if we keep spending beyond our means? Refer to the table opposite on page 165 for an analysis of the Canadian debt and deficit position when all three levels of government are included, prepared on the rather optimistic assumption that the deficit will plummet to zero by the year 2003. The combined debt (accumulated from year to year), even with a declining deficit (annual shortfall), will exceed $1 trillion by 1997. I find this alarming and suspect that the quest for a solution will be a long one, and in the end will perhaps be imposed not by Canadian politicians but those outsiders to whom we increasingly owe money.

One important rationale, therefore, for investing at least a portion of your resources in other currencies is to protect yourself against the risk that the Canadian dollar will drop in value during the coming years. I believe that there is a likelihood that this will occur at some point in the next 10 years or so, when our credit runs out, unless we get spending under control. And it would be wrong to believe that if this should occur we will be insulated from the effect as long as economically, if not physically, we remain in our own country. As a direct result of any such devaluation, the cost of imported goods will rise and, notwithstanding the corresponding fall in the cost of our exports and the stimulus that provides, our

DEBT AND DEFICIT POSITIONS: 1992

Federal, Provincial, Municipal Debt .... **$775 Billion**
Federal, Provincial, Municipal Deficit .... **$60 Billion per annum**

DEBT AND DEFICIT POSITIONS: 10 Year Projection

Year	Debt (billions of dollars)	Deficit
1993	835	60
1994	889	54
1995	937	48
1996	979	42
1997	1015	36
1998	1045	30
1999	1069	24
2000	1087	18
2001	1099	12
2002	1105	6
2003	1105	0

dependency on imported goods would likely lead to inflation at more than our hypothetical rate of 4% and dramatically reduce your purchasing power.

International diversification may well be a must for individual investors, and a good case can be made that the overall effect of having individual investors participate in the global economy would again be a positive one for the Canadian economy. If you achieve good investment returns internationally you will accumulate more personal wealth, pay Canadian taxes accordingly in most circumstances, not be a drain on the system and otherwise contribute to the Canadian economy.

In the face of Canadian reluctance to invest abroad, it is ironic to think that we have such a multi-racial country and yet we have so few economic ties and so little influence in the rest of the world, less than most of our friends, neighbours and competitors. This should not be the case.

The most basic rationale for diversifying your investments internationally is to reduce your risk by achieving higher returns when available, thereby outpacing taxes and inflation. Even the most conservative investment advisers are encouraging this trend to global investing, particularly in light of some mutual funds that are cropping up with regularity these days, mutual funds that specialize in international holdings, whether in one facet of international investing, one region or in a more balanced way.

Canadian tax law permits a certain percentage (increasing to a maximum of 20%) of your RRSP or IPP to be in international holdings. There is an ongoing debate between those on the political left who argue that permitting Canadians to get an RRSP or IPP tax break for a growing amount of foreign investment is a betrayal of our interests and those on the right who are interested in seeing the foreign content percentage increased. Nothing could demonstrate more graphically the differences of opinion as to how to manoeuvre Canada through the Great Restructuring.

It is not necessary to resolve this issue here other than to point out that, so long as the rules permit, a portion of your RRSP or IPP may be and should be invested internationally if superior rates of return can be achieved. Nor should you hesitate to let some of your other investment money see the world. Doing so is as easy as picking up the telephone and instructing your financial adviser accordingly. Global investments can be purchased, monitored and sold with facility in many international markets. Talk to your financial planner about it.

And don't overlook the fact that international investing can be fun. Studying and learning about opportunities as they crop up around the world can be fascinating on its own, and the thrill of having offshore profits cannot be denied. What could be more fun than to have a global portfolio to follow?

Please note, however, that not all international markets are well developed and that you should choose your investments with great care. In some cases, information is difficult to obtain and liquidity (the ability to sell investments quickly) may be a challenge. Not all currencies are stable and not all countries are stable politically. Some markets function differently from Canadian markets in terms of reporting standards and brokerage and other transaction costs. At least at the outset, I would recommend investing only in well established markets.

Preparing for Your Global Adventure

Canadian tax residents must pay Canadian income tax on their worldwide incomes. In other words, if you are a Canadian tax resident earning income outside Canada, you must declare and pay taxes in Canada on that income. This is true even if the foreign income is first taxed in the country in which it was earned.

Having said that, however, there is a foreign tax deduction and credit mechanism to assist you. It is complex and, at the risk of oversimplifying it, I will describe it here only in the most basic of terms. It generally grants tax relief, from Canadian taxes that would otherwise be levied on your investment income, for all or a portion of the taxes paid by you as a Canadian tax resident to the foreign country. Since the income was earned in the foreign country, that country has the first opportunity to tax the income according to its tax laws. Assuming that Canada has a higher rate of tax than the foreign country, which is most often the case, the remainder of the tax will be paid in Canada. But, as a result of the application of the tax rules, the total tax paid will generally not exceed the amount of tax due had the income been generated in Canada.

For example, if Canadian income taxes on $100 of income earned abroad were $50 and $15 had already been paid in the foreign country, the Canadian investor could claim that $15 against the $50, leaving $35 further to be paid in Canada. In this way, double taxation is avoided.

Further, the foreign jurisdiction in which the income is earned would generally levy a withholding tax, keeping in that foreign jurisdiction a portion of the income earned by you. For example, if $100 were earned, the foreign country would generally withhold a percentage of that $100 by way of withholding tax and the remainder would be delivered to the account of the Canadian investor. Although this percentage is frequently 25%, in the case of a country with a tax treaty with Canada, the withholding tax is generally reduced to 15% under the terms of the treaty. In such a case $85 would be released to the Canadian investor and the other $15 held by way of withholding tax. Canada has a tax treaty with most of the countries in which you would consider investing, tax havens such as The Bahamas, Bermuda and the Cayman Islands being notable exceptions. The list of tax treaty countries changes from time to time, so consult your financial adviser or Revenue Canada before investing.

In the case of a treaty country with a 15% withholding tax, you would claim a foreign tax credit for that 15% and would pay full Canadian tax less the amount withheld by the foreign country. In the case of a non-treaty country with a withholding tax of 25%, you would generally claim a foreign tax credit for 15% and take a deduction for the additional 10%, thereby saving a portion of that additional amount according to your marginal tax rate. If you are in the 50% tax bracket, you would save half of the additional 10%. Aside from certain brokerage or transaction fees that might be unique to the foreign jurisdiction, therefore, there is generally little or no tax advantage or disadvantage for a Canadian tax resident investing in a foreign jurisdiction, unless global tax planning is put in place. In the absence of employing certain global tax planning techniques, the main advantage of global investing is increased returns as global opportunities are exploited.

Next, global tax planning. There are those Canadian taxpayers, both individuals and corporations, who wish to plan their tax affairs to avoid or defer Canadian income tax, in whole or in part, on their international investments and business activities. To do this they must invest in international tax planning advice.

For an individual, there are three basic ways to avoid or defer Canadian tax on international investments, of which two are legitimate. The illegitimate method would be for you to stash investment funds in a foreign jurisdiction without informing Revenue Canada and earning and not declaring the income thereon accordingly. This is known as tax evasion. Not only is that an offence but it is a serious one. Those who indulge in such illegal activities often do so in non-treaty countries where there is little or no tax. Such Canadian taxpayers rely in these instances on the secrecy or confidentiality policies of banks and investment advisers in such jurisdictions. My advice is simple. Don't try it. If you do invest in those jurisdictions, declare every cent of your income to Revenue Canada.

The second approach is to change your tax residency, to cease to be a tax resident of Canada. Being a tax resident of Canada has nothing directly to do with being a Canadian citizen. It has to do with matters such as having substantial personal and business ties to Canada.

Sophisticated tax residency planning techniques have evolved that enable a Canadian tax resident to become instead a tax resident of another jurisdiction. It is sufficient for present purposes to point out that the assistance of a tax lawyer would be appropriate and that, in essence, these techniques are available to Canadians relocating on a permanent basis to another country and breaking their personal and business ties with Canada. It is obvious that only a limited number of Canadians will wish to take this approach and that it is generally taken not only for tax reasons but one or more other reasons as well, as to do so constitutes a substantial change in lifestyle.

The third approach is to remain a Canadian tax resident but structure your affairs in a manner that takes advantage of certain tax laws that allow you to become eligible to do business and invest globally without being required to pay Canadian income tax on each dollar as it is earned abroad. The wealthiest Canadian individuals (which will include you before long if you follow the strategies set out in this book) have been internationalizing their affairs for years. This is the domain of the international tax planning lawyer and is, I must point out, a complex and sophisticated field, certainly not something for the novice or even the experienced business person or investor to try without considerable professional assistance.

The basic approach for individuals with corporations has been to incorporate subsidiaries or foreign affiliates in other countries. The theory is that these foreign affiliates will be taxed in the country in which they were incorporated and through which they do business and will therefore not be taxed in Canada since they are not Canadian tax residents. It is sufficient to point out at this juncture that a complex series of tax rules has been enacted on this subject in Canada, but that basically it is possible for a Canadian to do business through foreign affiliates in certain circumstances without being subject to Canadian taxation. Professional advice is essential here.

For individuals wishing to invest and do business abroad, the traditional approach has been to incorporate an offshore corporation or establish an offshore trust, or both, and do business accordingly, since offshore corporations or trusts can be considered in certain circumstances to be separate taxpayers, not Canadian tax residents but rather tax residents of the jurisdiction where the corporations or trusts were created.

With respect to offshore corporations and trusts, the Government of Canada has enacted rules and subsequently tightened those rules over the past couple of decades. Further amendments should be anticipated over the years ahead. Nevertheless, there is still room for legitimate international tax planning in appropriate circumstances.

The objective of the government appears to be to strike a balance between collecting income tax on international operations and supporting Canadians who want to participate in the global economy without being placed in a disadvantaged position vis-à-vis Canada's competitors. The challenge over the past few decades has been to enable such global business and investment activities without having a stampede of investors create offshore corporations or trusts or whatever to earn income free of Canadian income tax.

As an aside, I anticipate, particularly in light of the report of the Standing Committee on Public Accounts tabled in the House of Commons on April 23, 1993 concerning offshore tax matters, that our tax laws will be clarified and tightened in the years ahead to limit the benefits of global tax planning to those Canadians genuinely interested in actively pursuing international business and investment. Smaller, passive investors simply seeking to save tax and those exploiting legal technicalities for the same purpose will find it increasingly difficult to accomplish their global objectives. That said, I also anticipate that the basic integrity of these tax laws will be preserved.

If you wish to internationalize your affairs and defer Canadian tax accordingly, note that it may be possible to do so, depending on the circumstances, but that professional guidance from an international tax planning lawyer—one with an emphasis on this specialized field—is a must. Note, however-er, that both the nature and cost of effecting and maintaining an international tax plan eliminate most smaller players and those interested primarily in making passive investments. In this regard, going global is by no means for everyone.

Note also that, unless you plan to change tax residency to a foreign jurisdiction (which most Canadians do not), Canadian taxation will eventually be payable as international income is repatriated to Canada and placed in your hands. In that regard, placing monies offshore in accordance with an international tax plan can be something like contributing to an RRSP except that the monies are not tax deductible when placed and there is no limit on the amount of money that may be put to work. Furthermore, the tax deferral is not necessarily absolute, as some level of tax is imposed by most foreign jurisdictions, albeit at generally lower rates than Canada's.

In summary, I believe that it is possible and desirable to internationalize your affairs to take advantage of global opportunities as they arise. In appropriate circumstances it may also be possible with international tax planning to defer taxes, at least partially, to facilitate your objective of achieving wealth.

8

PLANNING FOR THAT VERY RAINY DAY

THE FINAL PIECE IN YOUR STRATEGY to accumulate wealth is estate planning. It's a way to lock in some of the benefits of the steps we've just discussed, to preserve them for your family. If your wealth accumulation strategy is successful, you will have a sizeable estate, and much of it may be wasted unless you arrange your affairs to preserve it.

So just what is estate planning? This simple question is not easy to answer. Estate planning is a broad concept that can include, among other things, the law of wills, trusts, partnerships, corporations and income taxation, in the context of your death.

We have talked about life's first inevitability—taxes—and looked at ways to lessen the damage they can do. In estate planning, the objective is the same—we can't eliminate the inevitability of death, but proper estate planning can prevent that event from becoming a financial disaster for your family.

These two inevitabilities, death and taxes, are directly related, not in the sense that paying taxes will hasten your death, but in the sense that death can create the opportunity for government to take a large bite out of the wealth you've accumulated through a lifetime of effort.

Although it's true that we can't take our wealth with us when we die, it's also true that, in the absence of proper estate planning, we won't leave much behind. If this matters to you, read on.

Death and Taxes

Even in the absence of succession or estate taxes, as is the case in Canadian jurisdictions at the moment, it is not correct to assume that no taxes arise as a consequence of death. On the contrary, the estate of a deceased person must file a terminal tax return, which may result in the payment of substantial income taxes, particularly in the absence of proper estate planning.

As the law now stands, the most significant tax rule relating to the death of an investor, whether he or she has a will or not, is that the investor is then considered to have disposed of all non-depreciable capital property (land is a good example) and depreciable property (furniture, equipment, etc.) on death. The taxes that come due as a result of such a deemed disposition (sale) must be paid by your estate.

Let's take the example of non-depreciable capital property. Non-depreciable capital property, for the purposes of the Income Tax Act, is deemed to have been disposed of on death at a price equal to its fair market value at the time of death.

Assume that an individual has land with a fair market value of $1,000,000. Assume that this land was acquired years ago at $200,000. On death, the land would be appraised and the gain of $800,000 ($1,000,000 - $200,000) would generally be taxed as a capital gain.

At present, 75% of capital gains are taxable at the individual's marginal tax rate. In this example, $600,000 (75% of $800,000) would be taxed. Assume the highest marginal tax rate of approximately 50%. The income tax payable, therefore, would be $300,000 ($600,000 x 50%).

If there were no other assets except this $1,000,000 worth of land and there was no cash available from any other source, including life insurance, the heirs of the estate would have a problem. All or part of the land would have to be sold or mortgaged, if possible, to pay the tax.

Note that, where the heir is a spouse, this capital gain on the deemed disposition of the property can be deferred and the property transferred to that spouse without a capital gain if the spouse is a resident of Canada or in the context of a spousal testamentary trust. Testamentary trusts are discussed generally below.

The way to prevent this kind of adverse tax consequence on death is by effective estate planning, a discipline practised by a number of lawyers and accountants across the country. It is an area of growing importance in the face of increasing taxes.

Although this chapter is not a thorough analysis of the law of estates (it would take one or more large books to do that), I will briefly outline below a few of the basic tools of this increasingly important field.

ESTATE PLANNING TECHNIQUES

The Will and Testamentary Trusts

The will is the most fundamental document in your estate plan. An alarming percentage of Canadians do not have a will. Presumably, those without one intend to live forever. Otherwise, they will die intestate, in other words without a will.

You should take steps to avoid dying intestate, because in that circumstance it is the government that steps in and handles matters, not really an attractive prospect. The court will appoint an administrator of your estate and your property will be divided according to the provincial laws that apply, after appropriate taxes and expenses have been paid. No, you definitely should have a will, joint wills for you and your spouse in most circumstances.

Why not? In the case of a simple will it only takes a short visit to a lawyer's office and costs only a couple of hundred dollars for one that also includes some of the basic testamentary trust provisions referred to below. You should also resolve to review your will every so often, particularly as your circumstances change and the size of your estate grows, to ensure that your will reflects your intentions at all times. Every five years should be a minimum.

The fundamentals of a basic will generally provide for the appointment of an executor, a person you trust to handle the affairs of your estate on your death. You may also appoint one or more alternate executors, in case your first choice is a person who, at the time of your death, refuses or is unable to act. Many people appoint the lawyer who drafted the will as one of the possible executors on the reasonable assumption that he or she would be easy to locate and capable of doing the job properly. It is common for the first choice for the position of executor (called executrix when the person is female) to be the spouse or another close family member, preferably not someone much older than you are, as he or she must be alive on your death.

The will then provides that all funeral expenses and debts are to be paid out of the property of the estate. The remainder of the estate property, in a will with basic trust provisions, is placed in trust with a trustee to be dealt with according to the wishes of the deceased and in accordance with the trust powers granted to the trustee in the will. Often, the executor is also the same person appointed as the trustee, the person who administers the testamentary trust. This need not be the case; the two sets of responsibilities may be divided. You may wish to appoint someone else, another individual or a trust company, as trustee. Discuss this with your lawyer when planning your will, and remember that the law of wills varies from province to province.

Your remaining property is then dealt with according to your wishes as set out in your will. Actually, there are a few limits (some of which vary from one province to another) that restrict your ability to cut out your closest family members entirely, leaving them destitute, or to attempt through your will to control the behaviour of your heirs through the years and generations ahead. A court could determine, for example, that a bequest to your son on the condition that he not marry someone of a certain race or religion is void as it violates public policy, that is, our sense of fair play as a society.

But otherwise you are more or less free to deal with your property as you wish. Should you wish to put in some controls over how your estate is handled, the testamentary trust is a powerful tool. In fact, in the case of children younger than the age of majority, it is appropriate to place estate property in trust for them, to have the trustee manage the estate property for them until they are old enough to do it themselves.

Although we are now stepping out of the realm of the will that costs a couple of hundred dollars, take careful note that a will, particularly its trust provisions, can be used for a range of tax planning purposes, not for your personal benefit—a will and the trust provisions within it take effect only on your death—but for the benefit of your heirs. The larger and more complex your estate the more relevant this point is and the more important it is to select a lawyer with estate planning expertise. I have seen examples where literally millions of dollars are in the estate and bad planning or failure to plan leave this hanging in the balance. If you have gone so far as to accumulate wealth, estate planning is the next logical step.

If you are one of those readers who doesn't have an up-to-date will tucked away in your safety deposit box or your lawyer's safe (a safety deposit box or safe that your executor and major heirs know about so your will can be easily located—don't keep it in your house in case you die in a house fire!), please get cracking and prepare one. Don't let the fear of coming to grips with the inevitability of death stop you. I doubt anyone died sooner for having taken this basic step. Actually, the peace of mind that comes from looking after your affairs will be good for you.

Life Insurance

We saw under the previous heading concerning deemed dispositions on death that, without proper planning, serious cash flow difficulties can arise from the terminal tax return, difficulties that could be catastrophic for your heirs in some circumstances.

One way to prevent this from happening is to carry life insurance sufficient to handle any cash flow difficulties that might arise on your death. But how much life insurance should you carry for this specific purpose? Should this life insurance be in addition to the proceeds you wish to leave behind for other purposes, such as enabling the beneficiaries to continue without your annual income?

The answer to the last question is that we are dealing here with extra insurance, life insurance beyond that to replace your annual income and the like. We are talking about life insurance to handle estate cash flow shortages that may arise from estate taxes.

You'll need a qualified insurance agent on your team for this one, an agent who understands estate tax matters and who can assist you in evaluating your needs in this regard on an ongoing basis to ensure the preservation of wealth as it passes to the next generation.

The Estate Freeze

Before leaving the issue of estate planning, the concept known as an estate freeze should be mentioned. Basically, an estate freeze is an estate planning technique for deferring taxation on death. It is a particularly useful estate planning tool if you have substantial growth assets such as shares in an increasingly successful business.

In essence, effecting an estate freeze is something like dying prematurely, on paper. Through a series of corporate and trust manoeuvres, it's possible to freeze or lock the value of your estate, particularly the growth assets, so that the future growth in those assets during your lifetime will not be considered growth in your hands but rather growth in the hands of the next generation. Again, seek qualified legal expertise to explore the possibilities.

My advice for putting estate planning in place is basic. Make a list of all of your assets and visit an estate planning lawyer. Have a will prepared. Ask the lawyer whether setting up one or more trusts would be appropriate in your particular circumstances. If you have substantial growth assets, ask whether an estate freeze might be worthwhile. Ask about the tax consequences that might arise in the event of your death and whether life insurance might help the transition of assets from you to your heirs. Make a commitment to yourself to revisit these issues every few years as you travel the road to wealth accumulation, so that your personal estate plan is never out of date. Then get on with the job of accumulating wealth.

9

Summing Up

TEN YEARS AGO I attended a financial planning seminar and got all fired up about wealth accumulation. I had been practising law then for a couple of years and my income, although relatively modest, was better than it had ever been. We were starting to see a real light at the end of the tunnel. Our son was four and our daughter two. What better time to begin the process of accumulating wealth?

Most of those 10 years passed before we actually got started. I saw some (not many) of my clients doing it. I read books about it and kept promising myself we'd begin. But we didn't. Why not? The answer is, I'm not really sure. Probably it was partly being young enough and therefore far enough away from retirement to deny that something really needed to be done about it right away. And partly it was a genuine lack of understanding of the marvellous wealth accumulation possibilities just waiting at our fingertips if we would only reach out and grasp them.

I wish we had the time back, the chance to do that part of it again, because, in the course of the better part of a decade, hundreds of thousands of dollars passed through our hands. Had we invested 10% (or preferably 15% or more) of that amount, imagine how much further down the road to achieving wealth and financial security we'd be today.

But in my practice I meet individuals of all ages, especially those at or past middle age, who are filled with financial regrets and recriminations. Some get downright bitter, zeroing in on lost years and squandered opportunities. It can become yet another roadblock to getting on the wealth accumulation track. Don't let it happen to you. We didn't.

One day we just took the financial bull by the horns and did something about it. It felt good, satisfying. But why did we do it that day? Why not sooner, or later? And if I wrote a book about it, what special words could I use to help you take the same plunge, the same financial bungee jump. I'm not sure.

I remember a comment made by Zig Ziglar, that successful salesman and motivator, on one of his tapes to the effect that, as he wrote his first book he was rather overweight. In the book, which he printed in large quantity at his own expense and then proceeded to promote into a bestseller, he stated that he was thin, that he had lost many pounds. To promote his book with a straight face he had to lose the weight and keep it off, so he did. He put the pressure on himself and was motivated by it to take action. Maybe you can find a way to do the same thing for your tax and financial affairs.

Buy a calculator of the sort described in Appendix I and play with it. I found that helped. I've made tens of millions with mine, at least on the calculator's display screen. Try this one: multiply your gross annual income by the number of years you have left to work. You don't even need a calculator for that one. For many of you the answer will exceed a million dollars. Now ask yourself if you are prepared to let that much money slip through your fingers and end up with as little as you have now.

Remember, the key to achieving wealth is to free up some capital by good tax planning and, by paying yourself first, taking a reasonable percentage off the top every week or month. Then invest that capital in a tax sheltered environment to the extent the law allows. With the excess, allocate a portion to retiring non-deductible debt and a portion to investment. Take advantage of the capital gains exemption while it lasts. Take advantage of the small business deduction to the extent reasonably possible. As your wealth grows, look at adding an international component to take advantage of global opportunities as they arise.

To assist you in all of this, build a first rate financial planning team headed by a competent financial planner. But stay in charge yourself. Keep in touch with every aspect. Take nothing for granted. After all, it's your money and it's your life.

Don't let the naysayers grind you down. Always be mindful of the fact that accumulating wealth is good for you. It will ensure that you can live the kind of life you want to live, that you can get the most out of life. And remember, as you move forward on this path you will be putting dollars—eventually an incredible number of dollars—to work in the most productive ways, thereby increasing economic activity and wealth around you. Now that I think of it, you have a moral duty to do this. Don't let others dissuade you. If they try, attempt to convince them to fulfil their own duty by taking up the wealth accumulation challenge themselves.

The enemy is procrastination. It is the enemy within and is perhaps the greatest wealth destroyer of all. The time for action is now and the potential for achieving wealth is virtually unlimited.

APPENDIX
I

THE BUSINESS/
FINANCIAL CALCULATOR

THE SIMPLEST TOOL to calculate the effects of taxes, inflation and compound growth is a business/financial calculator. The one I use is one I bought at Radio Shack. The young salesperson informed me that everything I needed could be acquired for $30 in the form of a Radio Shack Business/Financial Calculator model EC-5010, a model similar to the Sharp Business/Financial Calculator model EL-731. Any business/financial calculator with the functions described below will suffice.

Permit me to give a simple example using this calculator. The relevant keys on this handy machine, once it is in "financial" mode and assuming you have trained it to round off to two decimal points for simplicity, are as follows:

- the number key, labelled "n";
- the interest key, labelled "i";
- the present value key, labelled "PV";
- the future value key, labelled "FV";
- the payment or contribution key, labelled "PMT";
- the compute key, labelled "COMP";
- the +/- key, labelled as "+/-".

Assume that an individual were able to set aside, say, $50 a week beginning at the age of 25 and retiring at the age of 65. How much money would be accumulated at 65?

Enter it this way.

- Enter $50 on the numeric pad.

- Strangely enough it is necessary to make the amount negative by pushing the "+/-" key (do this whenever you will be doing calculations using the "PMT," "PV" or "FV" functions. One of them must be entered as a negative number. Which one depends on the nature of the calculation. Trial and error will teach you quickly).

- Press the "PMT" key to enter this $50 as the regular payment. The screen will now show -50.00.

- Select an interest rate, say, of 12% by entering 12 on the numeric pad and, because we are dealing with weekly amounts, divide that 12 by 52 weeks in a year to give a weekly interest rate of 0.23. Enter the 0.23 as the weekly interest rate by pressing the interest key ("i" key).

- Next, enter the number of weeks: 52 weeks multiplied by

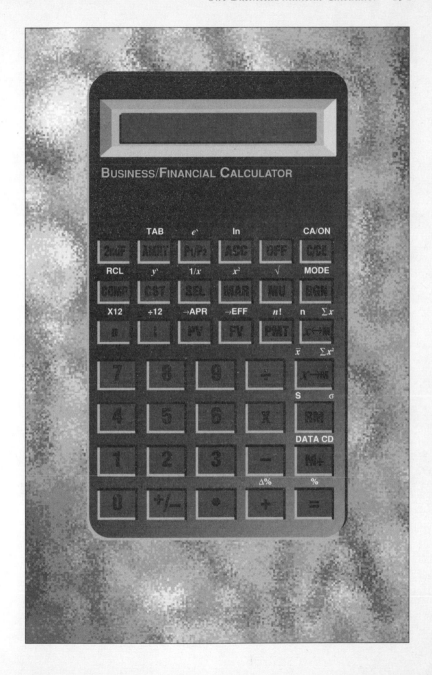

40 years equals 2,080 weeks. Enter 2,080 weeks by pressing the number key ("n" key).

■ Now, compute the future value by pressing the following two keys, one after the other: compute ("COMP" key) and future value ("FV" key).

■ The answer that will now appear on your calculator screen is $2,596,538.70.

In other words, if you begin at the age of 25 putting $50 a week away and earning compound interest of 12% per year, at the age of 65 you will have a nest egg of $2,596,538.70.

If you redo this example starting at the age of 35 but putting twice as much away, in other words $100 per week, the amount that will accumulate through compound interest by the age of 65 will be less, namely $1,536,025.50. Let us ask another question, therefore. How much would one have to put away weekly commencing at the age of 35 to have the same amount ($2,596,538.70) as a person who began putting $50 a week away from the age of 25?

Calculate it this way.

(Note that, between each set of calculations, it is necessary to clear the financial memory of the calculator completely. The financial part of the memory is cleared by pushing the "2ndF" and the "C.CE" keys one after the other at least once on my model. If you forget to do this the answers will be distorted.)

■ Enter $2,596,538.70 on the numeric pad and press the "+/-" key to make it negative.

■ Press the future value key ("FV" key).

■ Enter the weekly interest rate based on 12% per annum (12 divided by 52 weeks in a year equals 0.23). Enter this number by pressing the interest key ("i" key).

■ Enter the number of weeks in 30 years (52 weeks multiplied by 30 years equals 1,560, using the number key ("n" key).

■ Compute the weekly payment necessary by using first the compute key ("COMP" key) and then the payment key ("PMT" key) to find the answer: $170.57.

In other words, whereas a 25 year old could acquire $2,596,538.70 at 12% compound interest by the age of 65 by investing $50 a week, a 35 year old, being that much older and therefore having 10 fewer years to work with, would have to set aside $170.57 a week to achieve the same result.

Let us take just one factor, the interest rate. If one runs the prior example for our 35 year old on the assumption that 15% per annum were possible rather than 12%, the amount needed weekly would drop dramatically from $170.57 to $84.69 per week, a reduction of approximately 50%. Try calculating it for yourself.

In fact, try calculating all sorts of permutations and combinations. Run through every variable you can think of. I promise you will learn something valuable by trying, something that will help you in your quest to achieve wealth.

APPENDIX
II

IPP ASSET PROJECTION
FOR A PLAN BEGUN AT AGE 30

		IPP	
Year	**Age**	**Contributions**	**Fund at year-end**
1994	30	12,582	13,046
2000	36	20,418	148,444
2005	41	28,877	363,652
2010	46	41,022	735,568
2015	51	58,456	1,359,885
2020	56	83,486	2,385,929
2025	61	119,419	4,045,229
2030	66	164,208	6,687,753
2035	71[1]	189,400	10,676,964

		RRSP and GIC			
Year	**Age**	**Contributions RRSP**	**Contributions GIC**	**RRSP Fund at year-end**	**GIC Fund at year-end**
1994	30	13,500	(459)	13,997	(467)
2000	36	19,202	608	146,575	993
2005	41	25,096	1,891	345,555	8,323
2010	46	32,799	4,111	672,695	27,000
2015	51	42,868	7,794	1,196,558	66,055
2020	56	56,026	13,730	2,019,483	140,030
2025	61	73,224	23,098	3,293,498	271,929
2030	66	95,701	34,254	5,243,535	494,167
2035	71[1]	125,077	32,162	8,201,241	777,229

(1) IPP advantage over an RRSP at age 71 without considering the GIC Fund: $2,475,723 (30.19%). IPP advantage over an RRSP at age 71 if RRSP contributor has an additional GIC Fund: $1,698,494 (18.92%)

IPP BENEFIT PROJECTION
FOR A PLAN BEGUN AT AGE 30

Year	Age	IPP	RRSP and GIC	
		Annual Pension	Annual "Pension" RRSP	Annual "Pension" GIC
2019	55	189,006	161,225	10,735
2025	61	394,571	321,247	26,524
2030	66	729,617	572,056	53,912
2035	71	1,335,225	1,025,619	97,198

IPP ASSET PROJECTION
FOR A PLAN BEGUN AT AGE 35

IPP			
Year	Age	Contributions	Fund at year-end
1994	35	13,821	14,330
2000	41	22,330	162,319
2005	46	31,622	397,799
2010	51	44,962	805,016
2015	56	64,113	1,488,911
2020	61	91,607	2,613,260
2025	66	125,876	4,426,638
2030	71[1]	145,151	6,870,999

RRSP and GIC					
Year	Age	Contributions RRSP	Contributions GIC	RRSP Fund at year-end	GIC Fund at year-end
1994	35	13,500	160	13,997	163
2000	41	19,202	1,564	146,575	7,135
2005	46	25,096	3,263	345,555	22,225
2010	51	32,799	6,081	672,695	53,068
2015	56	42,868	10,623	1,196,558	110,825
2020	61	56,026	17,790	2,019,483	213,134
2025	66	73,224	26,326	3,293,498	384,845
2030	71[1]	95,701	24,725	5,243,535	603,433

(1) IPP advantage over an RRSP at age 71 without considering the GIC Fund: $1,627,464 (31.04%). IPP advantage over an RRSP at age 71 if RRSP contributor has an additional GIC Fund: $1,024,031 (17.51%)

IPP BENEFIT PROJECTION
FOR A PLAN BEGUN AT AGE 35

Year	Age	IPP Annual Pension	RRSP and GIC Annual "Pension" RRSP	RRSP and GIC Annual "Pension" GIC
2014	55	116,923	94,703	8,517
2020	61	254,897	196,980	20,789
2025	66	482,935	359,312	41,986
2030	71	859,264	655,739	75,463

IPP ASSET PROJECTION

FOR A PLAN BEGUN AT AGE 40

		IPP	
Year	Age	Contributions	Fund at year-end
1994	40	15,182	15,741
2000	46	24,430	177,559
2005	51	34,637	435,307
2010	56	49,290	881,302
2015	61	70,326	1,630,639
2020	66	96,547	2,858,847
2025	71[1]	111,295	4,502,525

		RRSP and GIC		
Year	Age	Contributions RRSP	Contributions GIC	RRSP Fund at year-end	GIC Fund at year-end
1994	40	13,500	841	13,997	856
2000	46	19,202	2,614	146,575	13,882
2005	51	25,096	4,770	345,555	37,495
2010	56	32,799	8,245	672,695	81,702
2015	61	42,868	13,729	1,196,558	160,002
2020	66	56,026	20,261	2,019,483	291,408
2025	71[1]	73,224	19,036	3,293,498	458,685

(1) IPP advantage over an RRSP at age 71 without considering the GIC Fund: $1,209,027 (36.71%). IPP advantage over an RRSP at age 71 if RRSP contributor has an additional GIC Fund: $750,342 (20.00%)

IPP BENEFIT PROJECTION
FOR A PLAN BEGUN AT AGE 40

Year	Age	IPP Annual Pension	RRSP and GIC Annual "Pension" RRSP	RRSP and GIC Annual "Pension" GIC
2009	55	68,242	52,500	6,243
2015	61	159,052	116,712	15,607
2020	66	311,893	220,320	31,792
2025	71	563,070	411,874	57,362

IPP ASSET PROJECTION
FOR A PLAN BEGUN AT AGE 45

		IPP	
Year	**Age**	**Contributions**	**Fund at year-end**
1994	45	16,676	17,290
2000	51	26,737	194,300
2005	56	37,948	476,509
2010	61	54,044	965,097
2015	66	74,106	1,783,164
2020	71[1]	85,391	2,889,692

		RRSP and GIC		
Year	**Age**	**Contributions RRSP**	**Contributions GIC**	**RRSP Fund at year-end**	**GIC Fund at year-end**
1994	45	13,500	1,588	13,997	1,618
2000	51	19,202	3,767	146,575	21,293
2005	56	25,096	6,426	345,555	54,268
2010	61	32,799	10,622	672,695	113,156
2015	66	42,868	15,619	1,196,558	212,470
2020	71[1]	56,026	14,682	2,019,483	338,983

(1) IPP advantage over an RRSP at age 71 without considering the GIC Fund: $870,209 (43.09%). IPP advantage over an RRSP at age 71 if RRSP contributor has an additional GIC Fund: $531,226 (22.52%)

IPP BENEFIT PROJECTION
FOR A PLAN BEGUN AT AGE 45

Year	Age	IPP Annual Pension	RRSP and GIC Annual "Pension" RRSP	RRSP and GIC Annual "Pension" GIC
2004	55	35,934	26,266	4,065
2010	61	94,135	65,615	11,037
2015	66	194,539	130,541	23,180
2020	71	361,375	252,550	42,392

IPP ASSET PROJECTION

FOR A PLAN BEGUN AT AGE 50

IPP			
Year	Age	Contributions	Fund at year-end
1994	50	18,318	18,993
2000	56	29,270	212,690
2005	61	41,586	521,766
2010	66	56,936	1,054,727
2015	71[1]	65,570	1,805,777

RRSP and GIC					
Year	Age	Contributions RRSP	Contributions GIC	RRSP Fund at year-end	GIC Fund at year-end
1994	50	13,500	2,409	13,997	2,454
2000	56	19,202	5,034	146,575	29,433
2005	61	25,096	8,245	345,555	72,692
2010	66	32,799	12,068	672,695	146,519
2015	71[1]	42,868	11,351	1,196,558	240,720

(1) IPP advantage over an RRSP at age 71 without considering the GIC Fund: $609,219 (50.91%). IPP advantage over an RRSP at age 71 if RRSP contributor has an additional GIC Fund: $368,499 (25.64%)

IPP BENEFIT PROJECTION
FOR A PLAN BEGUN AT AGE 50

Year	Age	IPP	RRSP and GIC	
		Annual Pension	Annual "Pension" RRSP	Annual "Pension" GIC
1999	55	14,988	10,412	2,070
2005	61	50,893	33,705	7,090
2010	66	115,068	73,389	15,985
2015	71	225,824	149,638	30,104

IPP ASSET PROJECTION
FOR A PLAN BEGUN AT AGE 55

IPP			
Year	Age	Contributions	Fund at year-end
1994	55	20,121	20,862
2000	61	32,053	232,889
2005	66	43,799	569,631
2010	71[1]	50,405	1,052,219

RRSP and GIC					
Year	Age	Contributions RRSP	Contributions GIC	RRSP Fund at year-end	GIC Fund at year-end
1994	55	13,500	3,311	13,997	3,372
2000	61	19,202	6,426	146,575	38,375
2005	66	25,096	9,351	345,555	92,023
2010	71[1]	32,799	8,803	672,695	160,684

(1) IPP advantage over an RRSP at age 71 without considering the GIC Fund: $379,524 (56.42%). IPP advantage over an RRSP at age 71 if RRSP contributor has an additional GIC Fund: $218,840 (26.26%)

IPP BENEFIT PROJECTION
FOR A PLAN BEGUN AT AGE 55

Year	Age	IPP Annual Pension	RRSP and GIC Annual "Pension" RRSP	RRSP and GIC Annual "Pension" GIC
1994	55	1,843	1,237	298
2000	61	22,716	14,297	3,743
2005	66	62,145	37,699	10,039
2010	71	131,587	84,125	20,095

IPP ASSET PROJECTION
FOR A PLAN BEGUN AT AGE 60

		IPP	
Year	**Age**	**Contributions**	**Fund at year-end**
1994	60	22,102	22,916
2000	66	33,747	253,664
2005	71[1]	38,801	584,840

		RRSP and GIC			
Year	**Age**	**Contributions RRSP**	**Contributions GIC**	**RRSP Fund at year-end**	**GIC Fund at year-end**
1994	60	13,500	4,301	13,997	4,381
2000	66	19,202	7,273	146,575	47,503
2005	71[1]	25,096	6,853	345,555	96,054

(1) IPP advantage over an RRSP at age 71 without considering the GIC Fund: $239,285 (69.25%). IPP advantage over an RRSP at age 71 if RRSP contributor has an additional GIC Fund: $143,231 (32.43%).

IPP BENEFIT PROJECTION
FOR A PLAN BEGUN AT AGE 60

Year	Age	IPP	RRSP and GIC	
		Annual Pension	Annual "Pension" RRSP	Annual "Pension" GIC
1994	60	2,193	1,339	419
2000	66	27,674	15,991	5,182
2005	71	73,138	43,214	12,012

IPP ASSET PROJECTION
FOR A PLAN BEGUN AT AGE 65

		IPP	
Year	Age	Contributions	Fund at year-end
1994	65	26,614	26,557
2000	71[1]	29,923	250,028

		RRSP and GIC			
Year	Age	Contributions RRSP	Contributions GIC	RRSP Fund at year end	GIC Fund at year end
1994	65	13,500	6,057	13,997	6,169
2000	71[1]	19,202	5,361	146,575	45,216

(1) IPP Advantage over an RRSP at age 71 without considering the GIC Fund: $103,453 (70.58%). IPP Advantage over an RRSP at age 71 if RRSP contributor has an additional GIC Fund: $58,237 (30.36%)

IPP BENEFIT PROJECTION
FOR A PLAN BEGUN AT AGE 65

Year	Age	IPP Annual Pension	RRSP and GIC Annual "Pension" RRSP	RRSP and GIC Annual "Pension" GIC
1994	65	2,827	1,490	657
2000	71	31,268	18,330	5,655

ABOUT THE AUTHOR

Ted LeValliant has been practicing business law for a dozen years, having graduated from the law school at the University of Saskatchewan in 1981.

Mr. LeValliant practices tax and distribution law, including domestic and international tax planning and domestic and international licensing and franchising, from his law office in Ottawa, with affiliate offices in North York (Toronto); London, England; Washington, D.C.; and Bridgetown, Barbados.

Mr. LeValliant is a member of the Law Society of Upper Canada and the Law Society of Saskatchewan. He also holds a postgraduate diploma in Legislative Drafting (legal writing) from the University of Ottawa.

Mr. LeValliant is the co-author of a book of legal puzzles entitled *What's the Verdict*, published by Sterling Publishing Co. of New York, and the author of *The Complete Guide to Franchising in Canada*, published by Macmillan Canada. His is a frequent speaker and is the editor of a tax effective financial planning newsletter, "The Wealth Accumulation Bulletin," published in Ottawa.